THE ORI
WARDEN

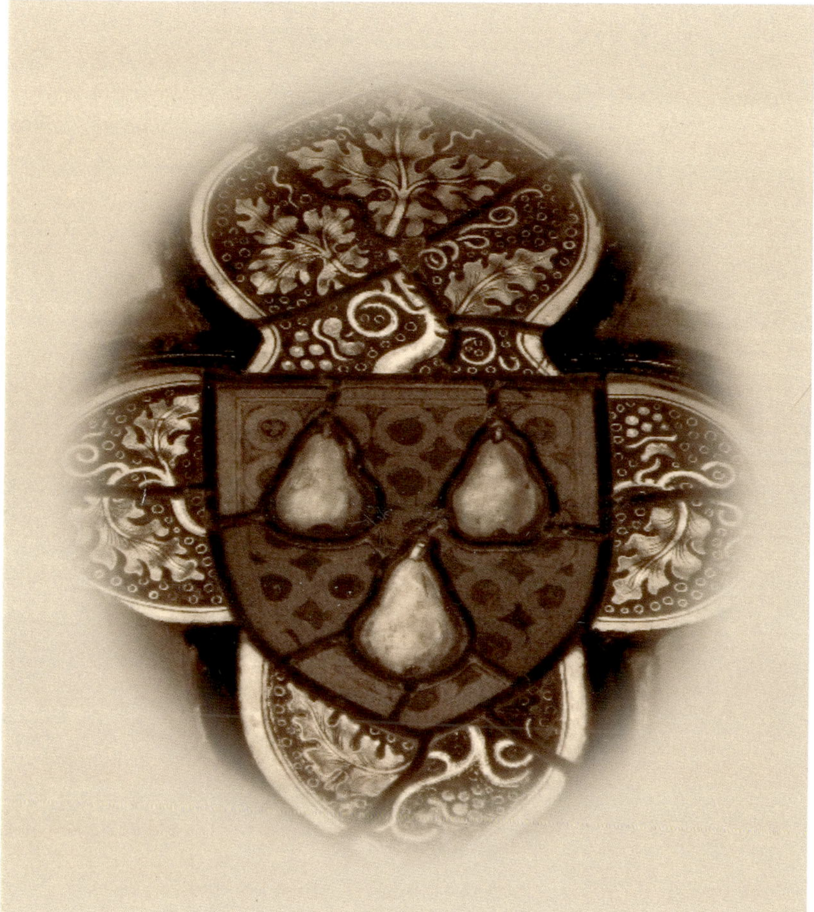

Margaret Roberts

First published in Great Britain in 2017
by Eventispress

Second edition (revised) 2018

A catalogue record for this book is available from the British Library.

ISBN: 978-0-9932608-4-1

Printed and bound by
Print2Demand Limited
Westoning
Bedfordshire

To Mum and Dad
Happy memories of home-made ginger cake topped with a sliced pear

Author's note

Founded in 1135, Warden Abbey in Bedfordshire was home to a thriving community of Cistercian monks until it was shut down by Henry VIII in 1537. The buildings were demolished by 1552, but the monks' legacy remained firmly embedded in the landscape. With the help of their lay brothers, they had tended two vineyards in the abbey precinct, where production would have peaked in the late 12th century. Climate change adversely affected grape growing towards the close of the 13th century, and natural disasters took their toll on manpower during the 1300s, yet the Great Vineyard and the Little Vineyard still appeared in the monastery's final accounts. Whether the land was used for anything other than pasture by then remains a mystery, but its original purpose was remembered on a map *c.*1750, which showed fields labelled 'Great Vineyard' (24 acres) and 'Little Vineyard' (16 acres). The site of the former abbey and adjoining farmland came into the hands of the Whitbread family in 1786, and having replanted part of the monks' Little Vineyard in 1986, Lady Jane Whitbread successfully revived the tradition of wine-making. Bedfordshire Rural Communities Charity took over responsibility for the vineyard in 2010, and I started volunteering there in January 2014.

Working outdoors, making friends and selling the end products (not to mention the occasional wine-tasting) were all part of the appeal. I've learned new skills, from vine pruning to layering, and from leaf stripping to grape picking, but more than anything, it's the monks' untold story that has been the greatest draw. My research has taken some unlikely turns, and curious to find out whether either the abbey or the nearby village of Old Warden had any connection with the warden pear, I headed off in a new direction. I'd like share my discoveries with you, so why not open a bottle of our wine before you read on?

Margaret Roberts
25 May 2017

Contents

1 Introducing the warden pear	1
2 The Bedfordshire connection	10
3 The orchard	20
4 Wardens in the arts	36
5 Time for tasting	43
6 Recipes	60
Acknowledgements	73

1 Introducing the warden pear

The power of pears

The story begins thousands of years ago, when the wild pear made a home for itself throughout continental Europe and across to north-west Iran. Farmers cherished the best seedlings, and records show that pear trees were being cultivated in Assyria (the area now occupied by northern Iraq, north-eastern Syria, south-eastern Turkey and the north-western fringes of Iran) in 2,000 B.C. The Ancient Greeks grew several varieties, but were outclassed by the Ancient Romans, who boasted at least thirty-five types of pear and three sorts of apple, which they nurtured along with plums, pomegranates, figs and quinces. Both civilisations valued pears for their flavour and medicinal qualities, but just as importantly, they regarded them as an aphrodisiac, dedicating the fruit to their goddesses of love, Aphrodite and Venus.

Nobody can be certain how or when pears reached our shores, but it is hard to imagine the Romans leaving their precious fruit at home, while they occupied Britain for 400 years. The monastic Orders probably helped to distribute fruit trees around Europe during the Middle Ages, and this was especially true of the Cistercians. Often referred to as the 'White Monks', they were said to have established a formidable reputation for their farming skills as early as the twelfth century, and whether or not they can take any credit, a dozen or more varieties of pear were acknowledged in Britain and France by the thirteenth century.

What was a 'warden'?

The *Oxford English Dictionary* unhelpfully describes *warden* as being 'of obscure origin', and the alternative spellings of *wardun, wardone, wardoun, wardane, wardyn/in, wardon, wardayne, wardeine* and *wardeyne* give nothing away. The dictionary goes on to speculate, that as the arms of the Cistercian abbey at Old Warden in Bedfordshire depicted three golden pears on a shield, the fruit might have taken its name from the monastery.

Anglo-Saxon and Anglo-Norman dictionaries, however, are more revealing. In Anglo-Saxon, *weardian* was defined as 'to guard, keep or defend', while in Anglo-Norman, *garder* and *warder* covered, among other things, 'to conserve, maintain and preserve'. This idea of keeping or preserving chimes perfectly with the warden pear, which was not only hard enough to survive storage throughout winter, but actually became sweeter towards the spring. In writing the first detailed grammar book of the French language during the sixteenth century, John Palsgrave hit the nail on the head, when he translated *wardon* as *poire de garde*, which simply meant 'keeping pear'.

The bookkeepers and physicians, food writers, poets and playwrights all left a legacy to prove that the word 'warden' was taken into common parlance more than 600 years ago. They sometimes used a capital 'w', but there was no consistency, and 'pear' was often seen as superfluous - the fruit was so commonplace that no explanation was needed. As far as most people were concerned, a warden was just a firm-textured cooking pear. However, in the seventeenth century, horticulturists began to attach 'warden' to the names of particular varieties of culinary pears, although their professional differences of opinion, exacerbated by the passage of time, have led to much confusion.

A fruit tree fit for a noble garden

The earliest written reference to warden trees is found in a twelfth-century document, when they were mentioned by English poet and theologian Alexander Neckam (1157-1217). In his compendium of scientific knowledge, *De Naturis Rerum* (*On the Nature of Things*), he described the plants, flowers, vegetables and herbs that should be included in a 'noble garden'. To these he added orchards of medlars, quinces, warden-trees, peaches, pears of St Regula, pomegranates, lemons, oranges, almonds, dates and figs.[1]

[1] Neckam used *volema*, a Latin word for 'pears' or 'wardens' in the original text. When Thomas Wright translated the book in 1863, he rendered *volema* as 'warden trees', possibly to differentiate them from the sweeter Pears of St Regula.

In 1375 wardens were recorded on the Petworth estate in Sussex, but there are no further details. An ancient deed of June 1383 is more enlightening, as it shows William Skeet the elder and Robert Rok of Matlask, Norfolk, transferring a property in that village to Roger Barfot, and his wife Margaret, of nearby Wickmere. In September 1385 the deed was endorsed with a memorandum to show that after Margaret's death, a nominal surcharge of three 'wardon peryz' had been imposed at the court of Bodham Hall in Wickmere. Payment was to be made annually at Christmas.

Accounting for fruit

The 1388 gardener's accounts for the Benedictine abbey of Abingdon[2] show that the monks generated 32s 6d from the sale of apples, wardens and nuts, while a 1449 document, relating to a grant of land at Tunstall near Faversham, Kent, refers to the profits of three pear trees called Jennettings and 'three trees called Wardens'. The *Household Books of John Duke of Norfolk and Thomas Earl of Surrey 1481-1490* recorded that on Friday 26 September 1483, 12d was paid to a woman who had provided 'wardones'. Almost fifty years on, the accounts of the keeper of Henry VIII's Privy Purse included payments to four people who had supplied wardens for the king: 6s 8d were given to a gunner's wife on 17 January 1531 for 'oranges and wardeyns' delivered to Yorke Place (now Whitehall), and 3s 4d were paid to a man bringing wardens on 12 April, which was very late in the season. The first of the new crop was delivered by a woman on 2 October, for which she received 5s, and the following year, the same was paid to a woman on 11 October 'in reward for giving a present of apples, wardens and quinces'.

It has to be hoped that King Henry VIII's secretary, Thomas Cromwell, was partial to wardens. On 15 December 1534 Sir Henry Penago presented him with 300 from Eynsford, Kent by way of apology that 'I am not able to do the King such service as I would', and on 2 April 1539, the accounts run by Cromwell's protégé, Thomas Avery, documented 12d given to a poor woman for 'bringing of wardens'.

---

[2] Abingdon was historically in Berkshire, but is now in Oxfordshire following changes to the county boundaries.

The warden goes to war

On 25 October 1415 the Worcestershire Bowmen went into battle at Agincourt under banners bearing their crest - a fruit-laden pear tree. This may have formed the basis of a story that wardens were part of the troops' rations, although given that it was remarkably early in the season, and the English army's campaign essentials would have prioritised wheat, malt, beans and peas, oats, oxen and sheep over fruit, it is hard to envisage the soldiers having enjoyed cooked pears beside the battlefield.

Wardens as part of a healthy diet

At a time when storing fresh food for the winter months was difficult, the warden came into its own as a source of vitamin C. Physicians, however, were united on one thing – raw fruit was bad for you. *Regimen Sanitatis Salernitanum* (printed in French in 1480, but possibly written much earlier) banned the eating of fresh pears, and this was endorsed in England, where, according to Thomas Cogan in *The Haven of Health* (1584):

> ...all manner of fruit generally fill the blood with water, which boils up in the body, as new wine doth in the vessel, and so prepares and causes the blood to putrefy, and consequently brings in sickness. So pears eaten raw make waterish and corrupt blood, and beside they engender wind, and so cause the colic. And therefore if any be so greedy of them, that needs they will eat raw pears, it shall be good to drink after them a draught of old wine of good favour, as sack or Canary wine. And this is the reason (as I think) of that saying which is commonly used, that pears without wine are poison.

Cogan added that roasted, baked or stewed pears were not unwholesome, and provided that they were ripe and 'well gathered', they would 'restrain and knit up the stomach and fortify the digestion if eaten after meat'. Reassuringly, he advised that 'the great pears, which *Virgil* named *Gravia volema*, in English pear-wardens, may be longest preserved and have chiefly the aforesaid virtues.'

According to the early sixteenth-century publication, *The regiment of life, whereunto is added a treatise of the pestilence, with the boke of children* by Goeurot, Phayer (1510?-1560) and de

Houssemaine (d. 1523), a powder of hartshorn, acorns, rose leaves, goat's claw,[3] pomegranate rind and galls was to be sprinkled onto the bottom of a child suffering from haemorrhoids. After a dash of powder had been strewn onto the gut (to improve the remedy's effectiveness) and a second dusting on the fundament, the offending area was to be bound with hot linen cloths. After this undignified treatment, the youngster was to be given quinces or a roasted warden to eat with cinnamon and sugar, although it is unclear whether this was intended as a pick-me-up, or thought to be of medicinal value.

The book also suggested various remedies for childhood dysentery. Powdered knotweed (or its juice) drunk in a posset was recommended, as was a plaster of knotweed, shepherd's purse, clay and plantain juice mixed with a little vinegar and wheat flour. Similarly, the rennet from a young, suckling kid could be given with the yolk of a soft-roasted egg (a real challenge for the cook). The child had to abstain from milk for two hours before and after this concoction, but could instead be allowed a roasted quince or warden with a little sugar and cinnamon.

The last illness of Cardinal Wolsey

In 1530 Cardinal Wolsey is reputed to have been eating roasted wardens at the moment when he was seized with his fatal illness. His gentleman-usher and biographer, George Cavendish described the situation:

> ...so that it came to pass at a certain season sitting at dinner in his own chamber having his board's end that same day, as he divers times had to accompany him, a mess of the earl's gentlemen and chaplains, and eating of roasted wardens at the end of his dinner, before whom I stood at the table, dressing of those wardens for him: beholding of him, I perceived his colour often to change and alter divers times, whereby I judged him not to be in health.

[3] Goat's claw may be a synonym for *glechoma hederacea* or alehoof (also known as cat's foot or turn-hoof), which Nicholas Culpeper described in *The Complete Herbal* (1649) as being used 'to wash the sores and ulcers in the privy parts of man or woman'.

The health benefits of wardens were acknowledged by physician Andrew Boorde, who said in his *Compendyous Regyment or A Dyetary of Helth* (1542) that they were nutritious roasted, stewed or baked, and comforted the stomach especially if eaten accompanied by preserved fruits. In the case of pestilence, he counselled the patient to avoid getting chilled, and to keep a fire in his room, steering clear of wood that was going to 'create much smoke'. The patient was also to shun wine, beer and cider, and eat stewed or baked wardens, if they were available. If not, the alternative was to have stewed or baked pears with preserved fruits.

Christopher Langton claimed in *An Introduction to Physicke* (1545), that lean rather than fatty meat was better for the stomach, as were pigs' trotters, pigs' ears, and the wombs of barren beasts. To his list of healthy foods, he added lettuces, parsnips, boiled cucumbers, cherries, mulberries, tender pears, oranges and quinces.

In medieval medicine, each human being was said to be formed from four basic humours: blood, phlegm, black bile and yellow bile. Yellow bile, or choleric humour, was believed to be associated with a peevish or irascible temperament, so when physician William Bullein, in his *Book of Simples* (1562), maintained that 'The red Warden is of greate vertue, conserued, rosted, or baken, to quench choller', it was in the belief that it would calm both the stomach and the mood.

In *Via Recta ad Vitam Longam* (1620), medical writer Tobias Venner questioned whether fresh fruit was beneficial. He concluded that 'Peare-Wardons' were not to be eaten raw, because they were hard to digest and bred a crude and flatulent humour. However they were good for an upset stomach, especially after drinking too much strong wine or beer. The reason, he observed, was that by sealing the mouth of the stomach, and by virtue of their 'cold and crude substance', they repressed and cooled the hot fumes that 'vaporated' to the head. Being baked or roasted, they were delicate and so not only beneficial for those in good health, but also for the sickly or ill, since they were very pleasant to the taste. Highly nutritious, they were easily digested and greatly comforting for a weak stomach.

According to John Parkinson in *Paradisi in sole paradisus terrestris* (1629), the red warden and the Spanish warden were suitable for everyone, such that, 'the Quince and the Warden are the only two fruits permitted to the sick to eat at any time'. Henry Butts, author of the Elizabethan book of dietary wisdom *Dyets dry dinner* (1599), thought otherwise. He believed that provided the fruits were fully ripe, sweet and pleasing to the taste, pears could be eaten in the autumn and winter by all *but* the aged and rheumatic. He considered that they should be used to stimulate the appetite, comfort a weak stomach, and force the jaws to 'raise and spit out phlegm' thereby assisting bowel movements. Perhaps a rather more reputable source was herbal practitioner, Nicholas Culpeper. In *The Complete Herbal* (1649), he said of the pear tree: 'All the sweet and luscious sorts, whether cultivated or wild, help to move the belly downwards, more or less'.

The death of Mr Quynbe

Narratives of the Days of the Reformation (published 1859) gave an account of an event that reputedly occurred in 1579, when a Mr Quynbe, who was imprisoned in the steeple of New College in Oxford, was asked by his friends what he would like to eat, as he was nearly dead from cold and starvation. He replied that 'his stomache was gonne from all meate excepte it wer a warden pye.' In jest, Mr Quynbe added that he would actually like the wardens responsible for his incarceration to be put in a pie, as it would do the Church more good, whereas 'other wardens from the tree can do me noo good at all'; at that point he turned his face to the wall, said his prayers and died.

1 Sources

Bullein, W., *The Booke of Simples* (1562), [pp. 13-14]

Butts, H., *Dyets dry dinner consisting of eight seuerall courses: 1. Fruites 2. Hearbes. 3. Flesh. 4. Fish. 5. whitmeats. 6. Spice. 7. Sauce. 8. Tabacco. All serued in after the order of time vniuersall* (London, 1599)

Cavendish, G., *The Life of Cardinal Wolsey* (printed 1641; repr. 1815 and 1905), p. 139

Cogan, T., *The Haven of Health* (1584), pp. 102-103

Collier, J.P. (ed.), *Household Books of John Duke of Norfolk and Thomas Earl of Surrey 1481-1490* (London, 1844), p. 464

Culpeper, N., *The Complete Herbal* (1649; repr. 1880), p. 263

Furnivall, F.J. (ed.), *The First Boke of the Introduction of Knowledge Made by Andrew Boorde ... a Compendous Regyment Or a Dyetary of Helth ...:* (Trübner, 1870; repr. 1906), pp. 284 and 291

Gairdner, J. (ed.), *Letters and Papers, Foreign and Domestic, Henry VIII*, 21 vols. (London, 1883), vol. 7, p. 575 [Entry 1545]

Gairdner, J. and R.H. Brodie (ed.), *Letters and Papers, Foreign and Domestic, Henry VIII*, 21 vols. (London, 1895), vol. 14 Part 2, 'August-December 1539, Miscellaneous, 1539', p. 329 [Entry 382]

"garder, v.a.5" [synonyms: 'gardeir, gardere, gardier, gardir, gardre, gardyr, gaurder; guarder, guardier, gwarder; warder, warder'], *The Anglo-Norman Dictionary Online Edition* accessed online: http://www.anglo-norman.net/

Goeurot, J., T. Phayer and N. de Houssemaine, *The regiment of life, whereunto is added a treatise of the pestilence, with the boke of children, newly corrected and enlarged by T. Phayre* (printed London, 1550)

Goodman, R., *How to be a Tudor* (London, 2015), pp. 233-37

Hancock, J.F. and G.A. Lobos, 'Pears', *The Future of Drylands: International Scientific Conference on Desertification and Drylands Research* (Tunisia, 2006) and (Springer, 2008), 304

Kirk, R.E.G. (ed.), *Accounts of the Obedientiars of Abingdon Abbey: the Gardener's Account 1388-9* (London, 1892), p. 53

Langton, C., *An introduction into phisycke wyth an vniuersal dyet* (London, 1545)

Maxwell Lyte, H.C. (ed.), 'Deed: A.9011', in *A Descriptive Catalogue of Ancient Deeds* (London, 1902), vol. 4

Morgan, J., *The Book of Pears* (London, 2015), pp. 10, 12, 51-52 and 58

Nichols, J.G. (ed.), *Narratives of the Days of the Reformation* (London,1859), p. 34

Nicolas, N.H. (ed.), *Privy Purse Expences of King Henry VIII November MDXXIX to December MDXXXII* (London, 1827), pp. 105, 126 and 265-66

Palsgrave, J., *Lesclaircissement de la langue francoyse* (1530)

Parkinson, J., *Paradisi in sole paradisus terrestris* (1629; repr. 1904), p. 594

Venner, T., *Via Recta ad Vitam Longam (A plaine philosophical discourse of the nature, faculties, and effects, of all such things, as by way of nourishments, and dieteticall obseruations, make for the preseruation of health with their iust applications vnto euery age, constitution of bodie, and time of yeare)* (London, 1620), p. 115

"warden, n.2", *Oxford English Dictionary* accessed online: http://www.oed.com/view/Entry/225645

2 The Bedfordshire connection

The village of Old Warden

There is clear evidence of the Romans having settled in and around Bedford. It is therefore possible that they introduced pears to the area long before the Anglo-Saxons invaded Britain in the second half of the fifth century. 1066 saw the arrival of the Normans, who recorded the Bedfordshire village of *Wardone* in the *Domesday Book* (1086); various alternative spellings were documented between the tenth and thirteenth centuries, including *Wardun, Waredon, Warden* and *Wardoun*. ('Old' was added by 1495.) As one of the highest points along the Greensand Ridge, *Wardone* is thought to mean 'watch hill', a term derived from a compound of the Anglo-Saxon *weard*, meaning 'ward, guard or watch', and *dún*, translated as 'down, moor, height, hill, mountain of'. This makes it unlikely that the village was named for its association with pears, although fruit growing was always popular, and in the parish register for 1727, the vicar listed orchard produce of apples, pears, plums, apricots, peaches and walnuts.

Did the monks of Warden Abbey cultivate pears?

Perched on top of the Greensand Ridge, Warden Abbey was home to a community of Cistercian monks from 1135 to 1537. There are no surviving accounts of pear cultivation on their home farm, but there is absolutely no doubt that they had fruit trees there. First called the Abbot's Garden Grange, the farm was later re-designated as the Farm of demesne lands, where two orchards were recorded in the post-dissolution accounts of 1537-38.[4] The same accounts show that after retiring as one of the abbey's servants, John Cowper lived rent-free in a tenement with an orchard in the hamlet of Warden Street (close to the abbey gate).[5]

---

[4] The home farm was recorded as *grang. Abbatiæ Gardini* in the monks' 1291 tax return.

[5] The hamlet of Warden Street grew up around the abbey gate and should not be confused with the present Warden Street, a road built in the late eighteenth century to the north of the former abbey precinct.

Following his death, sometime after December 1537, his dwelling and orchard were granted rent-free to Richard Honyley, described in the 1541-42 accounts as a retired clerk (clergyman). Another reference to fruit growing in 1537-38 relates to a tenement with a barn, orchard and adjacent piece of land in the parish of St Peter Dunstable, Bedford that a John Cockman had been renting from the monks. This cost him 26s 8d per annum, which was rather expensive.

Widowed around 1538, retired abbey servant Agnes Whanhope was still living rent-free in the Warden Street tenement that had been her home for many years. The property came with nothing more than a yard, but by 1541-42 she had taken on the tenancy of 'Seynt Annes Orchard', one of the monks' former holdings, for which she was due to pay 3s 4d in rent to the Crown bailiff. The name of the orchard had been carefully chosen to acknowledge that the Virgin Mary, who held a special place in the Cistercians' hearts, was the fruit of St Anne's womb. This particular orchard was not mentioned in earlier accounts, making it difficult to pinpoint its location, but it was undoubtedly close to Agnes's home as she was an elderly lady and would have wanted easy access. There is no indication of size, but comparison with other rental agreements of the same period suggests that it covered around two acres.

A mile to the east of the abbey, the monks held a property in Old Warden village called Orchard Grange, which the abbot rented out to farmer George Barnardiston on 19 July 1521 for a 36-year term at £12 per annum. This was an important asset. The abbot's manorial court was held there, probably twice annually by that time, and under the terms of his lease the tenant was obliged to provide refreshments for the officers of the court at his own expense. Post-dissolution leases of 1566 and 1574 expressly reserved half the crop of warden pears each year to the grange's landlord.

The Warden Abbey arms

The arms of Warden Abbey first consisted of three golden pears on an azure background, to which a golden demi-crozier with ram's horn had been added by the end of the fifteenth century. It is impossible to be certain when the abbey adopted the designs and there are no visible images in the parish church at Old

Warden, which the monks appropriated in 1376. A window depicting Abbot Walter Clifton was installed in 1380-81, but pears were not featured. The earliest available image of the arms without the crozier, features on a morse (a clasp used to fasten an abbot's cloak), which according to the British Museum, dates to between 1426 and 1475. Here the fruits are a pyriform shape with their stalks at an angle (one to the left and two to the right).[6]

Morse depicting the Virgin and child with the abbatial arms (1426/75), photo: © The Trustees of the British Museum

Pears were portrayed on the abbatial seal by 1449 [7] and the oldest surviving example, still without the crozier, is attached to a lease dated 1500, relating to lands in Haynes, Houghton Conquest and Maulden, Bedfordshire. By this time, the fruit had metamorphosed into a long pyriform shape with an exaggerated, bulbous base. The stalks were still shown at the same slanting angle, although each one now leaned to the right, and comparison with the Uvedale's St Germain pear highlights some remarkable similarities. The abbatial seal was updated to a grander design before 1537, when the image of three pears with a crozier was used on the abbey's counterseal bearing the legend, *SPES MEA IN DEO EST* meaning 'My hope is in God'.

[6] Pears can be described as flat-round, short-round-conical, conical, pyriform (the 'typical' pear shape), oblong/barrel, oval or long pyriform.

[7] Twenty abbatial seals were attached to a letter dated 28 December 1449 sent from the English abbots to the head of the Cistercian Order at Cîteaux. The seal of the abbot of Warden was distinguished by the words [probably around the edge] *Sigillum Iohannis ffrances abbatis de Wardona* [*Seal of John Frauncеys, abbot of Warden*]. The abbot was depicted together with two other figures, one on either side of him. Beneath his foot was a shield, and although the design was not described, it is reasonable to assume that, like later examples, it contained three pears.

Counterseal attached to the Deed of Surrender (1537), photo: TNA E/322/253, © M. Roberts

Uvedale's St Germain pear, photo: Alamy, © Anne Gilbert

The symbolism of the abbey's arms

The monks' choice of three golden pears, set against an azure background on a gold edged shield, was deeply rooted in early Christian beliefs. The number three itself had great significance, beginning with the three persons in the Godhead, Father, Son, and Holy Spirit. According to the Bible (Genesis, chapter 1, verses 9 to 11), God created dry land, grass and fruit trees on the third day, and three wise men brought gifts of gold, frankincense and myrrh to mark the birth of Jesus. Three crosses stood on Calvary when Christ was crucified, and He rose from the dead on the third day. Blue was traditionally associated with Mary, mother of Jesus, whom the Cistercians held in the highest regard. They believed that at the end of her earthly life, Mary was assumed into Heaven where she was crowned Queen, and gold was used to represent her queenship.[8]

[8] The shrine at Walsingham was founded in 1061 and the present statue of Our Lady of Walsingham has been modelled as closely as possible on the medieval version. Our Lady is depicted in traditional style wearing a blue robe edged with gold and a golden crown.

The arms of the abbey's founder

The arms of Warden Abbey's founder, Walter Espec, depicted three cartwheels, each with six spokes, on a plain shield. Stylistically they are in the same configuration as the three pears on the abbey's arms, but it is impossible to judge whether this had any bearing on the design chosen by the monks.

A pious man, Espec spent his professional career soldiering in the north of England, establishing Helmsley castle as his residence soon after 1120. He founded two religious houses in North Yorkshire (the Augustinian priory at Kirkham (1121/22) and the Cistercian abbey of Rievaulx (1132)) before establishing Warden as Rievaulx Abbey's senior daughter house. His arms are depicted on Kirkham Priory's gatehouse, which was rebuilt in the late thirteenth century.

It is possible that by selecting a pear, the monks were giving a respectful nod to nature's local bounty, but their choice is more likely to have had a theological basis. There are frequent references to fruit in the Bible, and although pears are never mentioned, they would have been seen as a symbol of the abundance of fruit and life in the Garden of Eden. Moreover, the Cistercians embraced Jesus as the fruit of the Virgin's womb and Mary has long been acknowledged in the Catholic prayer, based on the Gospel of Luke, when the archangel Gabriel told her that she was to be His mother:

> Hail Mary, full of grace.
> The Lord is with thee.
> Blessed art thou amongst women, and blessed is the fruit of thy womb, Jesus.
> Holy Mary, Mother of God, pray for us sinners, now and at the hour of our death. Amen.

Perhaps the arms also served as a visible reminder of The Fall of Adam and Eve in the Garden of Eden, where, despite God's warnings, they succumbed to temptation and ate the forbidden fruit from the Tree of the Knowledge of Good and Evil. This was a significant aspect of early Cistercian teaching, and during the first half of the fourteenth century, the monks of Warden underlined its importance by having a picture of The Fall crafted in a mosaic of floor tiles for the abbey church.

Although it is often illustrated as an apple, the Bible never mentioned the forbidden fruit by name and the early Christian theologian, St Augustine, chose pears for his personal analogy of The Fall. Augustine's work was greatly respected by the Cistercians, and the community at Warden would have been familiar with his *Confessions*, in which the author reflected on a shameful act from his teenage years. Out of sheer naughtiness, the young Augustine and his friends had stolen a large quantity of second-rate pears from a neighbour's orchard and thrown them to the pigs. It seems that the boys had incited one another to commit the theft and there had been no excuse for their behaviour. Augustine used the escapade as an example of pure sin - the desire only to do an evil act. The pear tree was his parallel to the Tree of the Knowledge of Good and Evil, and the orchard was a metaphor for the Garden of Eden. Peer pressure represented temptation and the stolen pears symbolised the forbidden fruit.

Where can you see warden pears on the abbey's arms?

Warden Abbey held a thirty-acre monastic farm at Millbrook near Ampthill [9] by 1161 and over the following two centuries, the monks acquired several hundred more acres in the vicinity. Sadly, debt forced the alienation of 320 acres at Millbrook in 1343 and a further 499 acres at Millbrook, Ampthill, Steppingley, Priestley, Flitwick and Coldcote (now Caulcott) in the late 1370s. It is therefore fitting to find the abbey's arms on a wooden, fifteenth-century roof boss in the north aisle of Ampthill Parish Church.

Walter Espec is commemorated in a series of Victorian stained glass windows in Helmsley Parish Church, and Warden Abbey's arms are illustrated in a light above two windows depicting his funeral (*Front cover*). Founded in 1835, Mount Saint Bernard Abbey in Leicestershire is the only Cistercian monastery in England today. Twenty English Cistercian coats of arms are depicted on the lead waterheads of the Abbey church, and although far from being an accurate representation, the arms of Warden are included. Tilty Abbey near Great Dunmow in Essex (founded in 1153) was the third of Warden Abbey's three daughter houses. Tilty's 'chapel without the gate' survived attacks by Cromwell's soldiers to become the parish church, and the west window (restored in 1981) acknowledges the links with the mother house in a stunning representation of Warden's arms.

Warden Abbey's arms: the myths

Local legend has it, that the arms reflected the pride of the abbey in its horticultural achievements, while the OED goes so far as to say that 'There can be little doubt ... that the arms were devised with punning intention'. Yet these suggestions do a grave disservice to the medieval Cistercians, a silent Order in which humility was a virtue and humour was actively discouraged.

A more bizarre hypothesis suggests that the choice was a gesture towards the Peruzzi banking family, whose crest bore one, or more probably, three golden pears in the early fourteenth century. Having taken out astronomical loans from the Peruzzi's during the 1320s, the monks failed to repay in full until 1345, by which time the bank had gone into liquidation.

[9] The landholding was confirmed in a charter of Henry II dated to 1160/61 and reconfirmed by Henry III. The charter was reissued on 14 December 1508 by Henry VII.

Restored fifteenth-century roof boss in
Ampthill Parish Church, photo: © M. Roberts

Lead water head on the
Abbey church at Mount St
Bernard Abbey,
Leicestershire,
photo: © M. Roberts

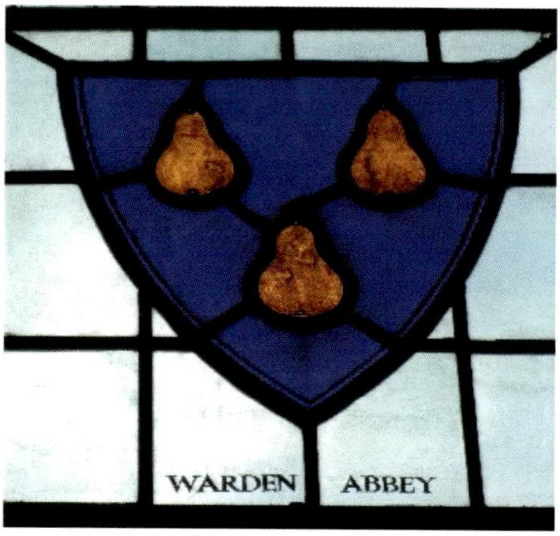

Parish Church of St Mary the
Virgin, Tilty, photo: © M.
Roberts

2 Sources

Bedfordshire Archives and Records Service, RO5/208 [Deed with seal attached]

Christianity Today accessed online: http://www.christianitytoday.com/history/issues/issue-15/and-saint-in-pear-tree.html

Dugdale, Sir William, [Translated by J. Caley, Sir Henry Ellis and B. Bandinel], *Monasticon Anglicanum: A History of the Abbies and Other Monasteries, Hospitals, Frieries, and Cathedral and Collegiate Churches, with Their Dependencies, in England and Wales; Also of All Such Scotch, Irish, and French Monasteries as Were in Any Manner Connected with Religious Houses in England*, 8 vols. (London, 1825), vol. 5, part 052, p. 369

English Cistercian Coats of Arms on the lead waterheads of the Abbey church, (The Saint Bernard Abbey Press,1998), image Number 2

Hunt, E.S., *The Medieval Super-Companies: A Study of the Peruzzi Company of Florence* (Cambridge, 1994), pp. 118-19

Lawson, S. (ed.), *Helmsley Castle* (London, 2004; repr. 2014), p.1

Maxwell Lyte, H.C. (ed.), *Calendar of the Patent Rolls Edward III*, 10 vols. (London, 1902), vol. 6 (1343-1345), p. 147 (entry dated 3rd December 1343) and *Calendar of the Patent Rolls Richard II*, 6 vols. (London, 1895), vol. 1 (1377-81), pp. 10-11 (entry dated 17 July 1377)

Maxwell Lyte, H.C. (ed.), *Calendar of the Patent Rolls Henry VII*, 2 vols. (London, 1916), vol. 2 (1494-1509), p. 616

McGinn, B., 'The Spiritual Teaching of the Early Cistercians', in *The Cambridge Companion to The Cistercian Order*, ed. M. Birkedal Bruun (Cambridge, 2013), pp. 218-232

Morgan, *The Book of Pears*, pp.266-67

Nicholls, Y. (ed.), 'Court of Augmentations Accounts for Bedfordshire – I', in *Bedfordshire Historical Record Society Vol. 63* (Bedford, 1984), pp. 81 and 93 (Clauses 107 and 124)

Nicholls, Y. (ed.), 'Court of Augmentations Accounts for Bedfordshire – II', in *Bedfordshire Historical Record Society Vol.64* (Bedford, 1985), pp. 150-52 (Clauses 429-31)

Old English Translator accessed online: http://www.oldenglishtranslator.co.uk/

Sheen, A., *Old Warden. An Archaeological Survey* (unpublished document dated 1977 held by Central Beds Council), appendix 5, notes that 'Old' had been added to 'Warden' by 1495. In the section on 'Domesday and afterwards', Sheen cited B.P.R. X A53-54 as his source of information on the Old Warden parish register 1727.

Talbot, C.H., (ed.), *Letters from the English Abbots to the Chapter at Cîteaux 1442-1521* (London, 1967), p. 39

The National Archives (TNA) E/322/253 Court of Augmentations: Surrenders of Monasteries and Other Religious Institutions / Warden Abbey Deed of Surrender dated 4th December 1537

Underwood, A., *Ampthill Parish Church History and Guide,* 7th edition (Ampthill History Forum, 2007), pp. 47 and 49

"warden, n.2", OED accessed online: http://www.oed.com/view/Entry/225645

"weard-dún, n.", *Bosworth-Toller* accessed online: http://bosworth.ff.cuni.cz/about

Wood, J. *et al.*, 'Horticulture', in *Northill, Old Warden and Southill: Parish Survey* (Bedfordshire County Council, 1988) [Unpublished document held by Central Beds Council]

3 The orchard

Were there different varieties of warden?

There are no records of wardens coming in different shapes and sizes until the early seventeenth century. However, as English poet and farmer, Thomas Tusser, made clear in *Five Hundreth Pointes of Good Husbandrie* (1573), different colours were available, with 'Wardens, white and red' featuring in his list of fruits to be set or removed during January. The first formal record of various types of warden was published in 1629, when John Parkinson (master apothecary, gardener and herbalist to King Charles I) recorded sixty-four kinds of cultivated pears in *Paradisi in sole paradisus terrestris*. His list included 'the Warden or Luke Wardes pear of two sorts, both white and red, both great and small',[10] but in his opinion, the Spanish warden was 'greater than either of the former, and better also'. He differentiated wardens from the Worcester pear, which he noted was 'blackish, a far better pear to bake (when as it will be like a Warden, and as good) than to eat raw; yet so it is not to be misliked'. The pear of Jerusalem he considered to be 'of a very good taste: being baked also, it is as red as the best Warden, whereof Master William Ward of Essex hath assured me, who is the chief keeper of the King's Granary at Whitehall'.

The distinctive, long pyriform pear, later referred to variously as Dr Udale's Warden, Pickering's Warden and Union, must have been a familiar sight in Bedfordshire by 1500, when it appeared on Warden Abbey's seal. However, it was not documented until the second half of the seventeenth century, when botanist and plant collector, Dr Robert Uvedale (1642–1722), was thought to be growing it in south-east England. In 1691, his splendid garden along the south side of Church Street in Enfield boasted many exotic plants and flowers, and six or seven greenhouses.

---

[10] Bedfordshire lore has it that a man named Warden (or Ward) who lived near the village of Old Warden, grew large quantities of pears and regularly attended fairs and markets in Bedford to dispose of them, which is how they became well-known in the area. According to Evelyn Cecil (1895), a Luke Warde was said to have introduced a cherry from Italy to England and the '*Cerasus Luca Wardi*. Luke Wards Cherry' was illustrated by Parkinson in *Paradisi in sole paradisus terrestris*. It has not been possible, however, to establish whether this Luke Ward(e) had any connection with pears.

When nurseryman John Rea published his catalogue in 1676, he included seven wardens: French Warden / Spanish Warden / Great Warden / Parkinson's Warden / Red [Roman] Warden / White Warden / Godboult's Warden. Also on the list were the Painted Pear, Tunip [*sic*] Pear, Canterbury Pear, Quince Pear, Bell Pear and the Black Pear of Worcester, all of which were good for baking.

The wild, gritty choak-pear or Choaky/Choake-Peare (*pyrum sylvestre*) was not unlike the warden in texture, but according to Parkinson, it was best left to the woods, forests, fields and hedges. The popularity of wardens began to wane as less gritty varieties of pear came onto the market in the late seventeenth century. By the 1680s, it was said of nurseryman and renowned tree supplier, Nicholas Parker of Chiswick, that unlike others, he would not substitute a rich French pear with a gritty choak-pear or Warden.

Almost 100 years passed before Philip Miller published the first edition of *The Gardeners Dictionary* (1724). Entries in Volume 3 discussed seventy-nine varieties of the best sorts of cultivated pears known by that time. He dismissed Choaky peares as unworthy of description, since they were 'seldom preserved in gardens'. With the development of new varieties, compounded by his attempt to standardise the naming conventions and descriptions of the pears, Miller unwittingly caused confusion. We can safely conclude that his Spanish Bon-crêtien[11] was synonymous with Parkinson's Spanish warden; so far, so good. However Parkinson's ambiguous account of the relative sizes of the Warden, or Luke Wardes pear, leaves room for doubt. Was the white warden 'great' and the red warden 'small', or were there both large and small variants of each colour? We don't know, although from his phrasing, the latter appears more likely. Furthermore, Parkinson took the view that the Black Worcester pear was different from any of the wardens, unlike Miller who now deemed Parkinson's Warden to be the same as the Black Pear of Worcester. Added to the mix, Miller's mention of a Union pear, otherwise called Dr. Uvedale's St Germain, leaves a muddle which we are unlikely to sort out.

[11] Many varieties contain Bon-crêtien (Bonchrétien, Bon Chrétien) in their name. There are various explanations, but I like Robert Hogg's suggestion in *The Fruit Manual* (1884), that the name derived from the Greek '*panchresta*', meaning 'all good' and referred to the fact that the fruit never rotted at the core.

The Gardeners Dictionary (1724)
by Philip Miller

No. 61 Bon-crêtien d'Espagne (The *Spanish* Bon-crêtien)
This is a large Pear, of a pyramidal Form, of a fine red or purple Colour on the Side next the Sun, and full of small black Spots; the other Side is of a pale-yellow Colour; the Flesh is breaking; and, when it is on a light rich Soil, and grafted on a Free-stock, its Juice is very sweet. It ripens in the Beginning of December, and will continue good a Month, or six Weeks. If this be grafted on a Quince-stock, it is very apt to be dry and stony: this is a very good Fruit for baking.

No. 62 *Poire de Livre* (The Pound Pear)
It is also called Gross Ratteau Gris (The Grey-rak'd Pear); and Poire d'Amour (The lovely Pear). In *England* this is called *Parkinson's* Warden, or the Black Pear of *Worcester*. This is a very large Pear, each of which commonly weights a Pound or more; the Skin is rough, and of an obscure red Colour on the Side next the Sun; but somewhat paler on the other Side; the Stalk is very short, and the Eye is greatly hollow'd. This is not fit for eating, but bakes or stews exceeding well; and is in Season from *November* to *Christmas*.

No. 80 The Union Pear; otherwise called Dr. Uvedale's St. Germain
This is a very large, long Pear, of a deep-green Colour; but the Side next the Sun doth sometimes change to a red as it ripens. This is not fit for eating, but bakes very well; and being a great Bearer, and a very large Fruit, deserves a Place in every good Collection. It is in Season from Christmas to April.

By the time that William Forsyth produced *A Treatise on the Culture and Management of Fruit Trees* (1802), the warden's fall from grace was apparent, since it was not amongst his six preferred winter pear varieties. However the Spanish red warden [*sic*] and Union pears figured in a supplementary list, as did the Black Pear of Worcester, with asterisks to indicate that he thought these the best for baking or stewing. This indicates that like Parkinson, and in contradiction of Miller, he considered wardens and the Black Pears of Worcester to be different.

Pears described as 'wardens' were well established in Scotland by 1822. Writing on the ancient orchards of Jedburgh, Thomas Shortreed observed that the town was very famous for its fruit. He listed twenty-five cultivars of pear growing there, including the White Warden or Monks' Pear, and the Grey Warden. He had a very low opinion of the latter, noting that 'the loss of the Grey Warden would not be matter of much regret, as it is a coarse and harsh pear'. He was much more complimentary about the White Warden, which he considered 'really of good quality, being mellow, and pleasant tasted when pared. It possesses the quality of never chilling the mouth when eaten in cold weather, like the Achan and other juicy pears'.[12] This begs the question: if it could be peeled and eaten raw, was it a warden in anything but name?

Starting in the late eighteenth century, a Mr George Lindley began to gather material to compile an account of the fruit trees and vegetables grown in the gardens of Great Britain. It took him some forty years, and in 1833 he eventually published *A Guide to the Orchard and Fruit Garden: Or, An Account of the Most Valuable Fruits Cultivated in Great Britain*, which was aimed at the American market. In Section VII, he listed six types of baking and stewing pears, namely the Bellissime d'Hiver, Black Pear of Worcester, Catillac, Double-Blossomed, Trésor and Uvedale's St Germain. Lindley shared Miller's approach to the types of pear, maintaining that Parkinson's Warden and the Pound Pear (but not the Pound Pear of Langley) *were* synonymous with the Black Worcester, as were the Livre, Gros Ratteau Gris, Grande Monarque and Groote Mogol. He too referred to the Spanish warden by its modern name of Spanish Bonchrétien.

---

[12] According to Robert Hogg in *The Fruit Manual* (1860), the Achan was 'An excellent Scotch dessert pear, this is perfectly worthless in the south of England'.

A Guide to the Orchard and Fruit Garden (1833)
by George Lindley

Black Pear of Worcester (Parkinson's Warden, Pound Pear)

Fruit very large, of a roundish turbinate figure, usually about four inches long, and three inches and a half in diameter. *Eye* small, placed in a wide and deep hollow. *Stalk* half an inch long, stout, inserted in a slight cavity. *Skin* rough, of an obscure red or brown colour on the sunny side, but more pale on the shaded part. *Flesh* very hard, coarse of an austere taste, but very good when baked or stewed. In use from November till February. This grows very vigorously on the Pear [rootstock], but does not succeed upon the Quince.

Spanish Bonchrétien

Fruit large, somewhat angularly pyramidal, about four inches long, and three inches in diameter. *Eye* small, with a short erect calyx, deeply sunk. *Stalk* one inch and a half long, inserted in an oblique, obtuse-angled cavity. *Skin* pale yellowish green, tinged on the sunny side with streaks of dull red, thickly covered with brown specks. *Flesh* white, breaking. *Juice* not plentiful, subacid, with a pleasant astringency. In eating in November and December.

Uvedale's St German

Fruit very large, of an oblong figure, tapering to the crown, but compressed between the middle and the stalk; its usual size is about four inches long, and three inches broad, but sometimes much larger. *Eye* wide, in a deep hollow. *Stalk* an inch long, bent, and rather deeply inserted in an oblique angular cavity. *Skin* smooth, dark green, and of a dull brown on the sunny side; but as it becomes matured it is of a red colour on a yellowish ground. *Flesh* white, hard, and a little gritty next the core, with an austere astringent juice, which renders it unfit for eating raw, but it is excellent for baking and stewing. In use from Christmas till April.

> This does not succeed on an open standard; but it may be trained as an espalier, where it has a warm aspect, when it will bear and ripen very well. It, however, deserves an east or south-east exposure, and if well managed it will grow to a very large size. I have gathered it of seventeen inches its greatest, and fifteen inches its least, circumference, weighing thirty-one avoirdupois ounces; but a Pear of this sort, sent from Mr. Maisson of Jersey, was exhibited at the Horticultural Society, December 19, 1826, which weighed forty-four ounces.

There finally seemed to be consensus by the second half of the nineteenth century, when nurseryman and author, Robert Hogg (1818–1897), agreed with Lindley. In *The Fruit Manual* (1860), Hogg described the Black Worcester (synonyms Parkinson's Warden, Pound Pear and Warden) as large and obovate[13] with green skin covered by rather rough, brown russet and a dull, red tinge on the side facing the sun. Hogg made no mention of the stalk.

Hogg described the Spanish Bon Chrêtien or Spanish warden (synonyms Bon Chrêtien d'Automne; Bon Chrêtien d'Espagne; Gratioli D'Automne; Gratioli de la Touissant; Saffran D'Automne; Vandyck) as a large and pyriform fruit, its greenish-yellow skin covered with cinnamon-coloured russet and 'a deep, lively red colour next the sun'. The slender stalk was 1½ inches (38mm) long and inserted 'without depression'. Its white flesh was 'fine-grained and crisp with a brisk flavour and fine musky aroma'.

For the pear listed as Uvedale's St Germain, Hogg included seventeen synonyms, including Dr Udale's Warden, Pickering's Warden and Union. He described the fruit as being very large, sometimes weighing over 3lbs (1.36kg). Pyriform or pyramidal in shape, it had smooth, dark green skin which changed to yellowish-green. A dull, brownish-red on the exposed side, it was dotted all over with bright, brown flecks and a few traces of russet. The 1-1½ inch-long (25-38mm) stalk was inserted into a small cavity. Available from January to April, the white, crisp and juicy flesh

[13] 'Obovate' is a botanical term generally used to refer to a leaf whose narrower end is at the base. In the case of a pear, it infers that the broader end is uppermost.

made it ideal for stewing. Evidently these pears were considered a step up from the other wardens, a point underlined by the Oxford University Press in *Notes and Queries July-December 1870*, which recorded that 'The improved sort [of pear] now grown is Uvedale's Warden, or Uvedale's St Germain. The first is often of enormous size'. Yet this is another instance of confusion, as the article implies that the two were different.

A warden's place in the garden

The earliest record of a garden design incorporating an orchard of warden trees dates to the late sixteenth century. The creator was Sir Thomas Tresham, a devout Catholic, who suffered a succession of fines and periods of imprisonment for his beliefs. Having been released from house arrest in 1593, he spent his time planning a lodge at Lyveden in Northamptonshire, one of two buildings that he conceived as a proclamation of his faith. Rushton Triangular Lodge, a folly begun in 1594 and completed in 1597, was rich in symbolism, and his belief in the Holy Trinity was represented everywhere by the number three. Lyveden New Bield (sometimes called New Build) was a summer residence built in the grounds of Lyveden Manor House, and this too was full of religious meaning. Tresham gave orders that there should be a bowling green to the north of the New Build. Immediately to the north of the bowling green, a 'new gardening quarter' was to be laid out in a geometric pattern. Defined by gravel paths, he envisaged the planting of 'quince, peach, damson trees etc'. For the area to the north of the gardening quarter and east of a moated orchard, Tresham proposed an orchard of warden pears, which he called 'my warden quincunx hills'.[14]

Not long afterwards, Gervase Markham offered advice on planting fruit trees in *The English Husbandman* (1613). Working on the assumption that the orchard could be divided into quarters, he suggested that the first should be planted with apple-trees, the second with pears and wardens, the third with quinces and chestnuts, and the fourth with medlars and service trees.[15]

---

[14] 'Quincunx' referred to an arrangement of five objects with four at the corners of a square or rectangle and the fifth at its centre, used for the five on dice or playing cards, and in planting trees.

[15] The *Sorbus domestica*, or service tree, is also known as the whitty pear. Now rare in Britain, it bears apple- or pear-shaped fruits, 1 inch (2-3cm) in length. The *Sorbus torminalis* has the common names of wild service tree, chequers, and checker tree. The fruits taste similar to dates.

However, if your orchard was 'of state and prospect, so that it containe eight quarters or more (according to the limitation of the earth) then you shall in euery severall quarter plant a severall fruit, as Apple-trees in one quarter, Peares in another, Quinces in another, Wardens in another, and so forth of the rest'.

Cultivation

We know from Thomas Tusser, that red and white wardens were to be set or removed during January, and the notebook belonging to Henry Oxenden of Barham, Kent dated November 1654, shows that he 'took up out of the Nursery at Maydeken 1 quince tree, 2 warden trees and 3 other Peare trees, and set them in Byton'. The best method of propagating fruit trees was, and still is, by grafting, as they cannot be reproduced 'true' to the original cultivar if they are grown from pips. Agricultural writer John Fitzherbert[16] discussed the best times in his *Book of Husbandry* (1534), recommending that pears and wardens should be grafted between St Valentine's Day and March 15th, 'bycause the sappe commeth sooner in-to the peare-tree and warden-tree, thanne in-to the apple tree'. He advocated grafting the pear or warden onto a pear rootstock, but if none were available, a crab-apple would do just as well. Some men, he said, used a whitethorn, but the resulting fruit was 'the more harder and stonye'.

The crop reaches maturity

According to Francis Bacon's *Sylva sylvarum* (1803), 'In September come grapes, apples, poppies of all colours, peaches, melo cotones,[17] nectarines, cornelians,[18] wardens, quinces... These particulars are for the climate of London...' In a chapter on natural history, he exhorted the reader to 'Experiment solitary touching the dulcoration of fruits' saying that 'Fruit groweth sweet by rolling, or pressing them gently with the hand; as rolling pears, damascenes, etc by rottenness, as medlars, services, sloes, hips, etc by time; as apples, wardens, pomegranates, etc by certain special maturations; as by laying them in hay, straw, etc and by fire; as in roasting, stewing, baking, etc.'

[16] There is debate over whether the book was written by John Fitzherbert himself or his younger brother, Anthony.

[17] According to the OED, 'melo cotones' can refer to any of several large, late-ripening varieties of peach, especially one with a thick covering of down; (also) a tree bearing such a fruit.

[18] The cornelian is the fruit of the Cornelian cherry tree (*Cornus mas*), a species of flowering plant in the dogwood family.

Generally pears are about ready to pick when they part from the branch as the fruit is lifted up; once they begin to drop from the tree, it is time to harvest them. Lawson's *New Orchard and Garden* (1597) advised that 'hard winter fruit and Wardens' were not fit to be gathered until after Michaelmas (September 29th), repeating the following advice proffered by Thomas Tusser just over twenty years earlier:

> The moon in the wane, gather fruit for to last,
> But winter fruit gather, when Michael is past:
> Though michers that love not to buy nor to crave,[19]
> Makes some gather sooner, else few for to have.
>
> Fruit gathered too timely will taste of the wood,
> Will shrink and be bitter, and seldom prove good;
> So fruit that is shaken, or beat off a tree,
> With bruising in falling, soon faulty will be.

Similarly, when John Evelyn published *Sylva* (1664), one of the most influential texts on forestry ever produced, he recorded eight types of apple and eleven pear varieties, which, along with bullaces, medlars and services, were in their prime during November. The Warden, he earmarked specifically for baking.

Gathering the fruit

The Husbandman's Fruitfull Orchard (1609) noted that wardens were to be gathered, packed, carried and laid (stored) in the same way as winter pears. It was more specific than other texts concerning when to gather the crop, explaining that timing depended on how the pears were to be used. If they were for sale or personal use, they were to be gathered as soon as they started to change, but still appeared to be no more than half ripe. Those left to ripen fully on the tree would ultimately rot sooner. If the pears were to be transported some distance, either by land or water, one of the fruits should be pulled from the tree and cut in half. If the core was hollow, they were to be gathered and laid in a heap, even if none of them were actually ready to drop. That way, they would ripen by themselves and make for good eating. Gathered any earlier, they would wither, shrink and 'eat rough', losing not only their taste, but also their appearance.

---

[19] Michers: robbers or petty thieves.

It was considered bad practice to beat the trees using poles to make the pears fall off, as the fruit bruised easily, and once damaged, it rotted more quickly. Consequently, the best method was to balance on a free-standing ladder, which did not even touch the tree trunk. The picker would use a basket, which, when full, he would lower to the ground using a line. By keeping the string still while the basket was being emptied, he could then pull it back up and finish the job without climbing up and down the ladder, or damaging the tree.

Any fruit falling to the ground, rather than having been gathered by hand, was not to be laid with the hand-picked fruit. There were two sorts of windfalls, one which fell because it was ripe, and being the better of the two, could be kept to bake or roast. The others had to be used immediately, or they would wither and come to nothing.

Carrying the crop

The fruit was to be placed in deep, wicker baskets, each with a capacity of four or six bushels, and carried between two men to the apple-loft.[20] If it had been gathered some distance from the loft, the bottoms of the wicker baskets were to be lined with green fern, the ends of which were drawn through gaps in the wickerwork to prevent the fruit from touching anything other than the soft fronds. For pears, straw could also be used. The tops of the baskets were to be similarly covered and a small cord drawn over it, to prevent the fruit from scattering, or jogging up and down, while it was being transported. In the case of pears, the fern actually helped to ripen them.

Storing the crop

General storage instructions for pears were included in the *Second Book, entreating the ordering of Orchards* (1577) by Conrad Heresbach, who observed that preservation methods included dipping the stalks in boiling pitch and then hanging them up, or keeping the pears in newly boiled wine, or in some sort of closed vessel. Some growers, he said, preferred to store the fruit in sand or flocks (left-over scraps of wool), while others covered them with wheat or chaff.

---

[20] Bushel: a measure of capacity equal to 8 gallons (equivalent to 36.4 litres), used for corn, fruit, liquids, etc.

Working on the assumption that there were several sorts of fruit in the orchard, *The Husbandman's Fruitfull Orchard* recommended that each type had to be laid separately. However, if this was impossible due to lack of space or too many varieties of fruit, those closest to one another in taste could be laid together in the first instance. On the basis that the newly-gathered pears were not sufficiently ripe, they could be laid in heaps on top of sweet straw, and as they ripened, the fruits could be uncovered and spread in thinner layers, so the air could pass through. Alternatively, if you did not want them to ripen, then you could lay them directly onto the floorboards. The temperature of the store was important. Too warm, windy or cold, and it could damage the crop, so a 'temperate place' with some air, but not too much, was ideal. Careful storage allowed the fruit to sweeten over time, and less sugar was needed for cooking.

The *poire de garde* lives up to its name

In the *English Husbandman*, Markham reconfirmed that the fruit was a good keeper, saying, 'your stone-Peare, Warden-Peare, and choake-Peare [are] those which indure longest', and in 1510, Abbot John Islip of Westminster was reportedly tucking into quinces, apples and warden pears at the beginning of the year. 1549 found civil servant John Coke crafting a fictional debate between the heralds of England and France, in which each side bragged about the advantages of his own country. On the subject of fruit, the English herald observed, 'England is a fruitful and plenteous region so that we have sum fruites whereof you have few, as wardeines, quynces, peches, medlers, chestnottes and other delycious fruytes serving for all seasons of the yere'.

The warden revived

By the early nineteenth century, recipe books only mentioned 'pears', even though they were clearly referring to the hard varieties that required lengthy cooking. The word 'warden' fell out of popular use by the middle of the century, and although not deemed obsolete by the OED, it must now be a close-run thing. So what became of the named fruits? The Spanish warden (Spanish Bonchrétien) seems to have disappeared, but happily others live on. The Black Worcester (Parkinson's Warden) is probably the best known, and interest in this ancient variety was revived by Shuttleworth College (part of Bedford College) at Old

Warden, Bedfordshire in 2012. It is available from several commercial sources who describe it as a moderately vigorous, spreading tree. Attractive in the autumn with colourful leaves and fruit, it is a reliable cropper with large fruit suitable for culinary use.

Black Worcester pears in Turvey Community Orchard, Bedfordshire, photo: John Warwick

Uvedale's St Germain (Dr Udale's Warden, Pickering's Warden) is only available from a very small number of specialist growers. It is marketed as a large, culinary pear from a vigorous and heavy cropping tree. The fruit is said to be ready for harvesting in October and can be stored for use throughout the winter months, but I have not had chance to put this to the test.

Catillac pears from Old Warden, Bedfordshire: at 4.33 inches (110mm) high (from the base of the fruit to the bottom of the stalk), and with a circumference of nearly 12.6 inches (320mm), the largest pear weighed in at 18.34oz (520g), photo: © M. Roberts

A ‘warden’ in everything but name, a Catillac pear tree has been identified in an orchard at Old Warden. According to research commissioned by Paul Labous of Shuttleworth College, genetic testing shows that although there are some similar alleles (each of two or more alternative forms of a gene that arise by mutation and are found at the same place on a chromosome), there is no obvious DNA connection between the Catillac and the Black Worcester. (The latter certainly does not keep as well.) Developed in France during the reign of Louis XIV (1643-1715), the Catillac was recorded in the UK by 1696. Lindley (1833) described it as:

> ...very large, of a broad turbinate figure, somewhat in the shape of a Quince; usually about three inches and half or four inches deep, and the same in diameter. *Eye* small, with a short neat calyx, placed in a deep and wide plaited hollow. *Stalk* an inch long, stout, curved, and a little obliquely inserted in a very small cavity. *Skin* yellow, and when well matured in a warm season, of a deep orange, with a red tinge on the sunny side. *Flesh* hard, with an austere juice. In use from December till April. This succeeds better on the Pear [rootstock] than on the Quince. The Catillac is a most excellent Pear for baking and stewing. The tree is very hardy, a handsome grower, and a very good bearer upon a common standard, and deserves a place in every choice collection of fruit.

Old Catillac trees are found all over Britain, but are rarely planted now and only sold in limited quantities by specialist growers, who describe it as a vigorous tree with a spreading and weeping growth habit, and large attractive blossom. Very hardy, it is a regular and heavy cropper. If you can find any of these pears, they are perfectly suited to medieval cooking techniques.

3 Sources

Amherst, A., *A History of Gardening in England* (London, 1896), pp. 187 and 260

Anon., *The Husbandman's Fruitful Orchard, For the true ordering of all sorts of Fruits in their due seasons; and how double increase commeth by care in gathering yeere after yeare: as also the best way of carriage by land or by water: With their preseruation for longest continuance. Etc.* (London, 1609), pp. 127 and 129-30, accessed online: http://www.gutenberg.org/files/29058/29058-h/29058-h.htm#HFOrchard

Bacon, F., *The Works of Francis Bacon: Sylva sylvarum (century IX-X) Physiological remains. Medical remains. Medical receipts. Works moral: Colours of good and evil. Essays or counsels civil and moral. Theological works* (Printed for J. Johnson, 1803), pp. 26 and 364

Bott, V., 'Gardening in Thames-side parishes 1650-1850; Nicholas Parker', *Nurserygardeners.com* (2010) accessed online: http://nurserygardeners.com/?p=70

Boulger, G.S., 'Uvedale, Robert (1642–1722)', rev. Anita McConnell, *Oxford Dictionary of National Biography* (2004) accessed online: www.oxforddnb.com/view/article/28042

Cecil, E., *A History of Gardening in England* (London, 1895), p. 9

Coke, J., *The Debate between the Heralds of England and France* (Paris, 1875), p. 117

Evelyn, J., *Sylva; or, A discourse of forest-trees, and the propagation of timber in His Majesties dominions. As it was deliver'd in the Royal Society, the XVth of October, CI)I)CLXII ... To which is annexed, Pomona; or, An appendix concerning fruit-trees in relation to cider, the making and several ways of ordering it* (London, 1664), p. 78

Fitzherbert, J., *The Book of Husbandry* (Trübner & Co, 1882), p. 88

Forsyth, W., 'On Pears', in *A Treatise on the Culture and Management of Fruit-trees: In which a New Method of Pruning and*

Training is Fully Described. To which is Added, a New and Improved Edition of "Observations on the Diseases, Defects, and Injuries, in All Kinds of Fruit and Forest Trees": with an Account of a ... (London, 1802), pp. 80-105 (p. 93)

Harvey, B., *Living and Dying in England 1100-1540: The Monastic Experience* (Clarendon Press, 1993), p. 61

Heresbach, C., *Four Bookes of Husbandry* (London, 1577), p. 85

Historic England List Entry on Lyveden New Bield accessed online: https://historicengland.org.uk/listing/the-list/list-entry/1001037

Hogg, R., *The Fruit Manual; containing the descriptions and synonymes of the fruits and fruit trees commonly met with in the gardens and orchards of Great Britain with selected lists of those most worthy of cultivation,* (1860), pp. 150, 170, 212 and 217, and 5th edition (London, 1884), p. 667

Labous, P., *The Bedfordshire Old Warden Pear: identification by DNA testing, propagation by grafting and bedding out* (Shuttleworth College, 2017) [Final report for the Heritage Lottery Fund]

Lindley, G. and J. Lindley (ed.), *A Guide to the Orchard and Fruit Garden: Or, An Account of the Most Valuable Fruits Cultivated in Great Britain* (London, 1833), pp. 275-77

Markham, G., *The English husbandman. The first part: contayning the knowledge of the true nature of euery soyle within this kingdome: how to plow it; and the manner of the plough, and other instruments belonging thereto. Together with the art of planting, grafting, and gardening after our latest and rarest fashion. A worke neuer written before by any author: and now newly compiled for the benefit of this kingdome* (1613), The Second Part of the First Book, chapter 1 'Of the Scyte, Modell, Squares, and Fashion of a perfect Orchard', pp. 35-36

Miller, P., *The Gardener's Dictionary,* 3 vols. (London, 1724). vol. 3. [Entries for pears are listed under PY]

Morgan, *The Book of Pears*, pp. 208-209

Orange Pippin: All about apples, pears, plums, and cherries - and orchards where they are grow accessed online: https://www.orangepippin.com/pears/catillac

Parkinson, *Paradisi in sole paradisus* terrestris, pp. 573, and 592-93

Rea, J., *Flora, Ceres & Pomona* (London, 1676), p. 202

Shortreed, T., 'Some Account of the Remains of the Ancient Orchards of Jedburgh', in *Memoirs of the Caledonian Horticultural Society* vol. 3 (1825)

Tusser, T., *Five Hundred Points of Good Husbandry,: As Well for the Champion Or Open Country, as for the Woodland Or Several; Together with A Book of Huswifery. Being a Calendar of Rural and Domestic Economy, for Every Month in the Year; and Exhibiting a Picture of the Agriculture, Customs, and Manners of England, in the Sixteenth Century* (1573), ed. W.F. Maver (London, 1812), pp. 19 and 85

White, W. (ed.), *Notes and Queries: A Medium of Intercommunication for Literary Men, General Readers, etc.* Fourth series vol. 6 (Oxford University Press, 1870), 124

4 Wardens in the arts

The oldest surviving literary reference to the warden is found in a late fourteenth-century poem called *The Pistill of Susan*. The poem recounts the biblical tale of Susanna and the Elders, (Daniel chapter 13) with various orchard fruits and nuts mentioned in the eighth verse. These include ‘wardons winlich and walshe notes newe’ meaning lovely wardens and fresh walnuts. In *Pur le Roy*, one of the minor poems of monk John Lydgate (c.1370–1449/50?), he describes how Henry VI was received in London after his coronation in France. The poem is lengthy, and we have to read as far as the fifty-third verse before finding his observation that ‘the frutis wiche more comon be, Quenyngez, pechis, costardes, *etiam* wardons’, a reference to popularity of quinces, peaches, custard apples and wardens.

The pear as a symbol in art

The 1511 image of *The Virgin and Child with the Pear* by the sixteenth-century artist, Albrecht Dürer, is one of his most beautiful images of the Madonna and Child. The infant’s hand is raised in a gesture of blessing and the pear, held by the Virgin Mary in her right hand, represents the sweetness of her soul.

Dürer’s 1526 oil painting of the *Madonna and Child with a Pear* is said to symbolically derive from a passage in the Bible that invites one to taste and ‘see how good the Lord is’. (Psalm 34, verse 8: ‘O taste and see that the Lord is good: blessed is the man that trusteth in him.’) For this reason, the pear may allude to the sweetness of virtue.

In Beaumont and Fletcher’s play, *Cupid's Revenge* (written between 1607 and 1612), there is an exchange between two courtiers after one of the other characters has just been beheaded. They are discussing the alternative forms of execution that might have been preferable, with Agenor asking, ‘Why how would you have had him died?’ This elicits the response from Dorialus, 'Faith I would have him roasted like a warden in a brown paper, and no more talked on’t.

The Winter's Tale

by William Shakespeare
(first performed in 1611, but not published until 1623)

In Act IV, Scene 3 of the play, the clown rehearses his shopping list:

> Let me see. What am I to buy for our sheep-shearing feast?
> …I must have saffron to colour the warden
> pies; mace; dates?—none, that's out of my note;
> nutmegs, seven; a race or two of ginger, but that I
> may beg; four pound of prunes, and as many of
> raisins o' the sun.

The silliness of his comments is lost today, but the audience would have known that wardens turned red when they were cooked, so there was no need for colouring, unless the cook chose to add mulberries or a little saunders.[21] Expensive spice would never have been justifiable, especially not one that would have turned the dish more yellow than pink.

The reputation of the warden during the early seventeenth century is evident from Henry Peacham's 1612 poem, *Emblems*. On describing an English fruit garden, he says:

> The Persian peach and fruitful quince,
> And there the forward almond grew,
> With cherries, known no long time since;
> The winter warden, orchard's pride;
> The philibert [hazelnut] that loves the vale;
> And red queen-apple so envide
> Of school-boles, passing by the pale.

---

[21] Saunders or Red Sandalwood (*Pterocarpus santalinus*) was widely used in medieval cookery as a red food dye, but can be highly unpleasant if not used correctly. By the nineteenth century cochineal (dried bodies of an insect used for making scarlet dye) was also popular and an 1809 recipe for Pear Compote suggested combining cochineal with red wine to give the pears 'a fine colour', while an 1820 recipe for Pears Red required 'two drops of pounded cochineal' to be added to the cooking water.

The Second Part of the Honest Whore
a comedy by Thomas Dekker
(published 1630, but probably written as early as 1605/06)

In Act I, Scene I, the following dialogue takes place between two men:

Lodovico. Do you hear? 1. 2. 3. S'foot, there came in 4. Gallants, sure your wife is slipt up, and the 4th man I hold my life is grafting your warden-tree.

Candido. Ha, ha, ha: you gentlemen are full of jest. If she be up, she's gone some wares to show, I have above as good wares as below.

Written in the 1680s, the English poet John Dryden's *Old Ballad of Bold Robin Hood* includes the following lines:

For there was hot venison and warden pies cold,
Cream clouted with hony-combs plenty:
And servitors they were besides Little John
Good Yeomen at least four and twenty.

Bellamira: or, The Mistris
an 'adult' comedy by Sir Charles Sedley (1687)

In Act III, Scene 1 the colour of a roasted warden is used as an insult. However it seems that even for its time, the play went too far. According to Richard Bevis (2014), there was a sharp, moral protest with objections to the playwright's callousness and the script's lack of redeeming features. The following snippet shows why:

Merryman. You shall see that this girl here is out of Ethiopia, of the Royal Blood there. I'll out lye him if possible.

Dangerfield. I bought a better for five Guineas, and gave her this morning to my Landlady's daughter.

Smoothly. She looks like a Warden Roasted in the Embers, or the outside of a Gammon of Bacon.

A humorous, twenty-two page poem called *The Art of Cookery* was published in 1708 by Dr William King. A lengthy piece, the reference to wardens comes not far from the end:

> Ox-Cheek, when hot, and Wardens bak'd some cry,
> But 'tis with an Intention Men should buy.
> Others abound with such a plenteous Store,
> That if you'll let them treat, they'll ask no more;
> And 'tis the vast Ambition of their Soul,
> To see their Port admired, their Table full.

Father Abbey's Will

An amusing poem by Harvard student, John Seccomb (1708–1792)

Pears were introduced to America by colonists in the seventeenth century and it is clear that wardens were a familiar sight judging by a poem written towards the middle of the eighteenth century. In fifteen verses, Seccomb describes how a Mr Matthew Abbey, who had long been a 'Bedmaker and Sweeper' at Harvard, might have written his last will and testament so as to leave everything to his wife, although this evidently didn't consist of much. Here are the first three verses:

> To my dear wife,
> My joy and life,
> I freely now do give her
> My whole estate,
> With all my plate,
> Being just about to leave her.
>
> A tub of soap,
> A long cart rope,
> A frying pan and kettle,
> An ashes pail,
> A threshing flail,
> An iron wedge and beetle.

Two painted chairs,
Nine warden pears,
A large old dripping platter,
The bed of hay,
On which I lay,
An old saucepan for butter.

One of the best known references to wardens comes in the ballad, *The Friar of Orders Grey*, from the comic opera *Merry Sherwood* by John O'Keefe (performed 1795). The friar is a plump and jolly soul who enjoys good-living, and chooses abstinence from warden pie as a form of penance in the second verse:

After supper, of heaven I dream,
But that is fat pullet and clotted cream;
Myself, by denial, I mortify-
With a dainty bit of a warden pye:
I'm cloth'd in sackcloth for my sin,
With old sack wine I'm lin'd within:
A chirping cup is my matin song,
And the vesper's bell is my bowl, ding dong.

A less familiar, but highly entertaining poem from early in the twentieth century is *Nell Cook! A Legend of the 'Dark Entry'*. Written by the Reverend Richard Harris Barham (under the penname Thomas Ingoldsby), it has the main protagonist using a Warden pie to commit murder. The story goes that pretty Nell Cook worked for a portly canon in Canterbury, but when his mistress came to stay, Nell 'bought some nasty Doctor's-stuff' and in a fit of jealousy, put it in a Warden pie to poison them. She achieved her aim, and both the canon and his mistress died. They were buried together in the church nave and Nell herself disappeared, but fearful noises were heard coming from beneath a paving slab in the passage beside the canon's door for a week afterwards. One hundred years later the slab came loose, and the masons sent to repair it found a woman's skeleton underneath with a small pitcher, and 'a mouldy piece of "kissing crust" as from a Warden-pie!' Nell was said to haunt the passageway every Friday night, and anyone who felt her breath died within the year. First to go were the three masons who discovered her bones…

4 Sources

Bevis, R.W., *English Drama: Restoration and Eighteenth Century 1660-1789* (London, 2014), p. 96

Birch, D. and K. Hooper, *The Concise Oxford Companion to English Literature* (Oxford, 2013), p. 554

Churchill, R.C. (ed.), *The Concise Cambridge History of English Literature* (Cambridge, 1970), p. 503

Collier, J.P. (ed.), *Old Ballads, from Early Printed Copies of the Utmost Rarity: Now for the First Time Collected, Issues 1-6* (Percy Society, 1840), 'Pur le Roy', p. 15

Dodsley, R. (ed.), *A Select Collection of Old Plays in Twelve Volumes* (London, 1825), vol. 3, 'The Second Part of the Honest Whore', p. 379

Dryden, J., *The first [-sixth] part of Miscellany poems: Containing variety of new translations of the ancient poets: together with several original poems,* 6 vols. (London, 1727), vol. 6, 'Old Ballad of Bold Robin Hood', p. 280

Ingoldsby, T., 'Nell Cook! A Legend of the 'Dark Entry', in *The Ingoldsby Legends or Mirth and Marvels* (Oxford, 1921), pp. 294-301

King, W., *The Art of Cookery; a Poem, in Imitation of Horace's Art of Poetry. By the Author of a Tale of a Tub [or Rather by Doctor William King]* (London, 1708), p. 20

Laing, D. (ed.), *Select remains of the ancient popular poetry of Scotland* (Edinburgh, 1822), 'The Pistill of Susan', p. 146

Sedley, Sir Charles and W. Ayloffe, *The Works of the Honourable Sir Charles Sedley, Bart: In Prose and Verse*, 2 vols. (1722), vol. 2, 'Bellamira: or, The Mistris', p. 123

Stedman, E.C. and E.M. Hutchinson (eds.), *A Library of American Literature: From the Earliest Settlement to the Present Time,* 11 vols. (New York, 1891; Bartleby.com, 2013), vol. 2, 'Father Abbey's Will', pp. 352-53

The Olio: Or, Museum of Entertainment ..., 3 vols. (London, 1829), vol. 3, 'Emblems', p. 398

The Universal Songster, 3 vols. (London, 1825), vol. 1, 'The Friar of Orders Grey', p. 73

The Works of Mr. Francis Beaumont, and Mr. John Fletcher: In Ten Volumes. Collated with All the Former Editions, and Corrected. With Notes Critical and Explanatory (J. and R. Tonson and S. Draper, 1750), vol. 9, p. 450

5 Time for tasting

When should wardens be served?

In *The Boke of Nurture* (1460/70), John Russell discussed the correct time to serve various fruits. He explained that plums, damsons, cherries and grapes might be offered before dinner, the main meal served in the middle of the day, while pears, nuts and strawberries had to be reserved until after the meat course. 'To ease the stomach' after supper in the evening, roasted apples and pears could be offered with *blaunche powder* dusted on top. Although Russell did not say so, the 'roasted pears' would, without doubt, have been wardens.

Powder Blanch (*blaunche powder*)

Thomas Cogan, in *The Haven of Health* (1584), published a recipe for a very good Blanch powder to 'strew upon roasted apples, quinces or wardens, or to sauce a hen . . .' The ingredients were two ounces of sugar, a quarter of an ounce of ginger, and half a quarter of an ounce of cinnamon, beaten together into a powder. Other cooks varied the flavour by adding a little nutmeg, or by warming the sugar and mixing in a little rose or damask water.

The *Book of Carving* (1508) provided instructions to senior servants in the very grandest of households on how to carve and serve at feasts throughout the year. Honoured guests dining between Michaelmas and Christmas would expect to be offered two courses of meat, unless the meal fell on a fasting day, when three fish courses would be presented. In the third of these (eaten standing up once the table had been cleared, or even in a separate room), the diners might anticipate spiced wine served with bream, perch, whelks, pears with sugar candy, or perhaps pears and quinces in syrup, figs, raisins, dates topped with minced ginger and wafers. Parsley roots, according to Nicholas Culpepper, helped the digestion, facilitating one 'to break wind, both in the stomach and bowels', and 'to open the body'.

Early in the seventeenth century, Hugh Plat, who wrote extensively on the art of preserving, conserving and candying, suggested that ladies might like to carry sweetmeats to quench their thirst when out riding. 'To make a paste to keep you moist', he recommended that stoned prunes and dates were beaten in a mortar, together with a roasted warden. The mixture was then placed into moulds, and left to dry in the oven after the bread had been baked. The addition of ginger, he maintained, would elevate the portable snack into a banquet dish.

By Tudor times, 'banquet' meant sweets, cakes, cheese, nuts and fruit with a glass or two of spiced wine, in contrast to a feast, which was a large meal. Writing *The English Huswife* (1615) not long after the close of the Elizabethan age, Gervase Markham elaborated on the preparations necessary for a banquet. He first described the sequence in which the prepared dishes should be organised in the kitchen, ready to be taken through to the dining hall. His list included 'wardens baked, raw or roasted'. (By 'raw' he may have been referring to whole, uncooked fruits preserved in syrup.) Markham went on to give detailed instructions concerning the order in which the dishes were to be delivered to the table:

> You shall first send forth a dish made for show only, as beast, bird, fish or fowl, according to invention: then your marchpane [the forerunner of marzipan], then preserved fruit, then a paste [a confection of sugar and spices], then a wet sucket [citrus fruits preserved in syrup], then a dry sucket [candied fruit], marmalade, comfits [sweetmeats made of some fruit or root preserved with sugar], apples, pears, wardens, oranges, and lemons sliced; and then wafers and another dish of preserved fruits, and so consequently all the rest before: no two dishes of one kind going or standing together, and this will not only appear delicate to the eye, but invite the appetite with the much variety thereof.

Dyets dry dinner consisting of eight seuerall courses (1599)
by Henry Butts MA, fellow of Corpus Christi College in Cambridge

Not content with simply repeating the usual medical advice on edible plants, fish and meat, Mr Butts was keen to promote pertinent conversation at the table. Get him on the subject of pears and he would bombard you with etymology. He would tell you that the English name Peare is derived from the Latin Pyrum or Pyrus, and that Pyrus comes from Pyramis (pyramid), because both the pear tree and the pear itself 'somewhat resemble that figure or proportion'. The pear tree, he might try to explain, 'aspireth and riseth with a kinde of Conus in the top', while the fruit 'pointeth toward the stalke; and his broad crowne representeth the basis'. [If it helps, draw a sketch to make sense of his explanation.] Dining companions, if they hadn't managed to divert him onto something less confusing, would learn that the Italians called their best pear, the Bergmot. 'Mot' he would reveal, 'is a Peare, and Beg signifies Lord or Master in the Turkish tongue, whence they borrowed it. As we say a Pome-roy from the French'.[22]

John Murrell, in *A Delightful Daily Exercise for Ladies and Gentlewomen* (1621), added a little more detail on 'A bill of Service for a Banquet'. He advocated serving your 'banqueting stuffe' in bowls of silver or gilt, or on glass plates. Each one was to contain two or three different fruits, but wet and dry were not to be put together in the same dish. Preserved wardens found a place on his list of fifty-one suggested banquet dishes. Murrell also mentioned an alternative, the 'Bill of Service for a Banquet on the Dutch fashion', again with two or three sorts of fruit in every bowl, and reiterated the instruction on keeping wet and dry elements apart. For this sort of banquet, he recommended forty-five possible dishes, including a Marmelate of Wardens.

John Parkinson (1629) echoed the accepted view that pears should be served at the end of a meal, not so much for the health benefits, but to allow the host the opportunity to show off his crop:

[22] Dr Henry Butts later became vice-chancellor of the University of Cambridge and committed suicide in 1632 while suffering from depression. The 'Pyra. Story for Table-talke' complements information on how to choose, use and prepare pears in *Dyets Dry Dinner*.

'...the most excellent sorts of pears [and other fruits] to make an after-course for their master's table, where the goodness of his orchard is tried. They are dried also, and so are an excellent repaste, if they be of the best kinds, fit for the purpose'.

In *The Compleat Cook's Guide* (1675), Hannah Woolley suggested serving a Warden Pye or Tart as part of a bill of fare for 'Autumn or Harvest'. This would have been an impressive occasion, when food was at its most plentiful. Her recommended first course consisted of a capon and white broth, a Westphalia ham with pigeons, a grand salad, a neat's tongue (cow or ox tongue) and udder roasted, a powdered (salted and smoked) goose and a turkey roasted. This would be followed by a potato or chicken pie, roasted partridges, larks and chickens, 'a made dish' (a fancy dish of various ingredients, depending on the cook's skill for its success), a warden pie or tart, and custards. Indeed wardens might well have featured in the 'made dish', served up preserved, baked, as a 'marmelate', or in syrup.

An alternative serving suggestion

By the late nineteenth century, Uvedale's St Germain pears (aka Uvedale's warden) were making their mark not only in England, but also in France, where they were known as Belle Angevine. No longer confined to their role as a mere cooking pear, they were so enormous compared with their peers, that they were turned into dining table centrepieces, or even shop window displays!

Cider or perry?

Whether wardens were ever used to make perry has gone unrecorded, but Parkinson observed:

> Perry, which is the juice of Pears pressed out, is a drinke much esteemed as well as Cyder, to be both drunke at home, and carried to the Sea, and found to be of good use in long voyages. The Perry made of Choke Peares, notwithstanding the hardnesse and evil taste, both of the fruit when it is greene, as also of the juice when it is new made, doth yet after a few moneths become as mild and pleasant as wine, and will hardly bee knowne by the sight or taste from it.

Wardens, baked* or roasted

(Recipes for dishes marked * are found at the end of the book.)

In the days of wood fires, food was roasted by direct exposure to, but not necessarily in or over, the heat source. Baking, on the other hand, was carried out in a dry heat. To bake bread for example, wood was first fired in the oven, and once the oven had reached the correct temperature, the charcoal was scraped out and the dough put in to bake.

It was well-known that wardens needed several hours' cooking to make them palatable, but on the plus side, the flesh kept its shape rather than dissolving into mush. Written in about 1393, household manual *Le Ménagier de Paris* (*The Goodman of Paris*) noted that as pears freshly picked at the beginning of the season (October and November) were hard and tough, they should be boiled in water. However, as they 'dried out and softened from the dampness of the weather' during the winter months, it was better to roast them over coals come February and March.

In terms of taste, Parkinson was right when he declared that 'the red Warden and the Spanish Warden are reckoned among the most excellent of pears, either to bake or to roast'. But for more attractive results, baked wardens were the better option, as their flesh changed to deep pink or red. Gentle stewing produced equally tempting dishes, but fruit roasted in the direct heat of an open fire shrivelled up and turned dark brown. Raphael Holinshed's *Chronicles of England, Scotland and Ireland* (1587) confirmed this, saying that if saffron was taken up before Midsummer or the beginning of July, the heads would 'shrink like a roasted warden'.

In 1420 Master Chiquart Amiczo, chief cook to Amadeus VIII, Duke of Savoy, compiled a book on the art and craft of cookery, which was effectively Europe's first true cookbook. Dictating his recipes to one of the duke's secretaries, M. Amiczo recommended baked pears as one of several dishes suitable for the sick. His recipe for *Les poyres cuytes sans brase ne eaue* (literally as 'Pears cooked without direct heat or water') began by instructing the cook to put the pears into a good earthenware pot. The pot was to be plugged with new wood, placed onto hot charcoal and covered with more coals.[23] Having been left for an hour or so, the pot was uncovered and the pears checked to see whether they were done. If not, they were left until they were ready, and then served to the patient on fine, silver dishes.[24]

Peers in Confyt (Pear confit),* Peris in syrippe (Pears in syrup)* and Warden compote*

A recipe for 'Peers in Confyt' (pears poached in red wine and finished in a syrup of sweet wine) is found in *The Forme of Cury,* compiled around 1390. They would have been just one of many dishes in the course served at the end of the meal, known in the medieval period as the void, which later became the banquet. It now makes a delicious dessert and I have included an updated version in the *Recipes* section.

As the source of her recipe for 'Peris in syrippe', the Honourable Alicia Amherst cited *A Book of Kokery*, a fifteenth-century collection of recipes aimed at aristocratic households. She added that at Henry IV's wedding feast in 1403, pears in syrup were served during the same course as venison, quails, sturgeon and fieldfare. As the taste of the period was to mix sweet and sour notes in the same dish, this was not sweet like the syrup we know today.

Compote (from the Old French *composte*) consists of fruit salad or stewed fruit, often in, or with syrup. The recipe in *A Book of Kokery* shows that it was sweeter than the pears in syrup. The compote's popularity endured, and according to Mrs Maria Wilson in *The Complete Confectioner, Or, Housekeeper's Guide* (1800), 'it was thought that there were many ladies in England who considered it no degradation to their character, in descending to recommend to their domestics whatever may be either useful or ornamental at their tables'. She observed that ladies would find 'a considerable reduction in their domestic expenses by attention to the valuable recipes contained in this Treatise', which included a recipe for a Compote of baked Wardens. The method was to 'bake your wardens in an earthen pot with a little claret, some

[23] The high water content of the new wood reduced the risk of it catching light.
[24] There are some rather odd translations of this recipe online, which involve inverting the cooking pot, a technique that does not appear in the original instructions.

spice, lemon peel, and sugar; when you use them, peel off the skin and dress them in plates, either whole or in halves; then make a jelly of pippins [apples], sharpened well with the juice of lemons, and pour it upon them; when cold, break the jelly with a spoon, and it will look very agreeable upon the red pears'. This was something of an improvement over an earlier version (*c.*1760) when wardens were stewed in a pot with a pewter lid, which turned them into 'Purple Pears' because the metals (tin, copper and sometimes lead) leached out from the pewter, making the dish into a serious health hazard.

In her nineteenth-century recipe for cooking whole, peeled pears, confectioner, Mrs Frazer of Edinburgh took preparation to a new level, by making a small hole in the eye-end of each fruit with an ivory bodkin (presumably so as not to stain the flesh) and picking out the seeds.

Chardewarden

'Charde wardoun' (literally 'flesh of warden) is described in the *Dictionary of Medical Vocabulary in English, 1375–1550* as a preserve made from the pulp of wardens, with the addition of spices, honey and pulp of quinces. This was actually a fruit cheese or paste similar to the present-day Spanish *membrillo*, as opposed to our modern jam-like conserves. Similar pastes were made from other fruits and the name altered accordingly, for example *chardequince*. A recipe dating to about 1450 usefully gave the proportions as 30 wardens to 10 quinces. To make charde wardoun, *A Book of Kokery* recommended boiling wardens in either wine or clean water, before grinding them in a mortar and straining to remove the liquor. The pulp was to be put into a pot with sugar, clarified honey and cinnamon, and brought to the boil. It failed to record how long the mixture was to be left on the fire, before being removed and allowed to cool. Raw egg yolks were used as a thickening agent and ground ginger added before serving, although the yolks were left out during Lent, when the pulp was boiled until thickened, possibly helped by the addition of rice flour.

During the Tudor and Stuart periods, quince preserve was known simply as marmalade (from *marmelo*, the Portuguese word for quince). No further explanation was considered necessary. If, however, the 'marmalade' was made from anything other than quinces, the fruits had to be specified in the recipe title. John Partridge's work, *The Treasurie of Commodious Conceites and Hidden Secrets* (1573), has a recipe 'To make marmalade of damsons or prunes', which he said could be adapted for wardens, pears, apples and medlars, services, checkers or strawberries, or indeed any combination, as you saw fit. To make the preserve, the fruits were boiled until soft and then forced through a coarse boulter (a piece of cloth used for sifting or straining), before being re-boiled with sugar.

Hugh Plat's recipe for a Marmelade of Quinces or Damsons (1609) helpfully notes the relative proportions of fruit pulp to sugar. The method was:

> When you have boiled your quinces or damsons sufficiently, strain them. Then dry the pulp in a pan on the fire. When there is no water left and it begins to thicken, mix in two pounds of sugar to every three pounds of pulp. This marmalade will be white marmalade and if you desire more colour, put your sugar and your pulp together as soon as the pulp has been passed through the strainer and let them both boil together. That way it will be the colour of ordinary marmalade, like 'unto a stewed warden', but if you dry your pulp first, it will look white, and need less sugar. You will know when it is thick enough by putting a little into a saucer and letting it cool before putting it into a box.

Preserved whole wardens

Published in 1545, *A proper newe booke of cokerye contained* simpler and cheaper recipes than *A Book of Kokery*, but the ingredients would still have been beyond the means of all but the most prosperous households. Its final recipe was 'For to make wardens in Conserve', a delicious-sounding dish created by making a syrup of one quart of good rumney (a sweet wine of Greek origin, popular in England especially during the fifteenth and sixteenth centuries), a pint of clarified honey and 1lb or ½lb of sugar and bringing them to the boil over the fire, before allowing the mixture to cool. This was regarded as a multi-purpose syrup, which would keep for a year or two.

The cook was then to clean (but not peel) twenty or so wardens and remove the 'bark' [the stalk and the eye]. These were placed in good red wine until they were well soaked and tender, but not to the point where they were saturated. The wardens were then drawn through either a cloth or a strainer, placed into an earthenware pot or glass jar and covered completely with the syrup to prevent the fruit from going mouldy; the quantity of syrup was down to the cook. Ground spices such as cinnamon and ginger were added, before the vessel was boxed and the wardens kept until they were required. There is no mention of cooking and therefore we have to assume that the double-soaking and lengthy storage were enough to make them edible.

Tarts with and without covers

Fruit tarts were evidently the latest thing towards the end of the sixteenth century, and Thomas Dawson included a recipe for a tart of wardens in *The Good Huswife's Jewell* (first edition 1585). The wardens were to be baked twice. First the fruits were cooked whole in a pie and then removed, quartered and cored, before being placed into a pastry tart case with a little sugar. More sugar was sprinkled over the top with some cinnamon and ginger, and then the tart was baked, uncovered, in the oven. A separate pastry lid was prepared - having the lid baked separately made it a tart with a cover, not a pie. Once the second bake had been completed, the rim of the pastry case and the underside of the lid were buttered to ensure that they adhered to one another as the cover was placed on top. More sugar was sprinkled over the tart before serving.

In *A Book of Cookrye Very Necessary for all such as delight therin…newlye enlarged* (1584), a recipe for 'Tartes of Quinces without covers' suggests wardens as one of the ingredients. The method was to 'Straine your Quinces with some wine, when they be boiled tender, and an apple with them, or two or three Wardens, straine them and season them with Sugar, Sinamon and Ginger, and so make tarte without a cover'. Printed in *The gentlewomans companion* (1673), Hannah Woolley's recipe for Warden-Tarts sheds light on the quantities:

> Take twenty good Wardens, pare them and cut them into your Tart, and put to them two pounds of refined

Sugar, twenty whole Cloves, a quarter of an Ounce of Cinamon broke into little bits, and three races of Ginger pared and sliced thin; then close up the Tart and bake it; it will require five hours baking; then ice it with a quarter of a pound of double refined Sugar, Rosewater and Butter.

Mrs Maria Wilson's recipe (published 1800)

To make paste for a standing crust

Mrs Wilson's recipe is striking, in that she insists on working the pastry once it has gone cold:

> To a peck of flour[25] put six pounds of butter, lay your flour in a large dish, make a hollow in the middle, put your butter in a saucepan of water on the fire, and when the butter is all melted take it off, and put it into the flour hot, and with a wooden spoon or stick, work it all together, then with your hands work your past quick, and pull it all into little pieces, till it is quite quite cold, then work it up into a stiff past, and form it into what shape you please, and build your walls for a standing pye.

Warden pies*

Warden pie was regarded as a real treat in the sixteenth century, although unlike Mr Quynbe, making a pun about wardens (his gaolers) as opposed to wardens (the fruit), would not have been at the forefront of most people's minds in their dying moments. Gervase Markham's 1615 recipe for a warden or quince pie is the tastiest I have tracked down:

> Take the fairest and best wardens, and peel them, and take out the hard cores on the top, and cut the sharp ends at the bottom flat; then boil them in white wine and sugar, until the syrup grows thick: then take the wardens from the syrup into a clean dish, and let them cool; then set them into a coffin, and prick cloves in the

[25] Peck: a unit of capacity for dry goods equal to a quarter of a bushel, now equivalent (in Britain) to two imperial gallons (approx. 9.09 litres).

tops, with whole sticks of cinnamon, and great store of sugar, as for pippins; then cover it, and only reserve a vent hole, so set it in the oven and bake it: when it is baked, draw it forth, and take the first syrup in which the wardens were boiled, and taste it, and if it be not sweet enough, then put in more sugar and some rose-water, and boil it again a little, then pour it in at the vent hole, and shake the pie well; then take sweet butter and rose-water melted, and with it anoint the pie lid all over, and then strew upon it store of sugar, and so set it into the oven again a little space, and then serve it up. And in this manner you may also bake quinces.

Hannah Woolley published a recipe for a Warden or Pear-Pye in her book *The Accomplish'd lady's delight in preserving, physick, beautifying, and cookery* (*c.* 1670) and an almost identical one was found in a collection of recipes belonging to Diana Astry of Bedfordshire (*c.* 1700). Both ladies opted to bake, rather than boil, the wardens before putting them into the pastry case.

Moyse (moise)

A moyse was generally made from stewed apples, but Thomas Dawson included a recipe for a quince or warden moyse in *The Good Huswife's Jewell*. First the fruits had to be roasted, then peeled and pulped before sugar, cinnamon and ginger were mixed in. Although the recipe fails to mention it, the cook would know that the mixture had to be thickened with breadcrumbs or rice flour, so that it would hold its shape when cut. To serve, the moyse was plated, smoothed with a knife and sprinkled with sugar before a small nick scored was in the top.

For an apple moyse, the fruit was roasted, peeled and strained into a dish. A further dozen apples were peeled and cut into a pan, with a dash of white wine and a knob of butter, before being boiled until they were 'as soft as Pap'. After a little stir, they were strained with some roasted, peeled wardens, before sugar, cinnamon and ginger were added. To serve, the moyse was to be made into diamond shapes, laid in the roasted apple sauce, and some sugar sprinkled over the top.

Sweet fruit pastes

Pastes were designed to be firm and they could be made into elaborate shapes with the judicious use of moulds. The flavour would have been more delicate than the moyse, since the fruit was boiled rather than roasted, and whereas the moyse was served soon after it was made, the baked paste could be stored until required. These fruit pastes are also known as fruit cheeses.

Markham used quinces in his recipe for a paste of Genoa, but he said that you could also use pears, apples, wardens, plums of all kinds, cherries, barberries, or indeed whatever other fruit you pleased. The quinces were boiled until soft, and then beaten in a mortar together with refined sugar, cinnamon, finely sieved ginger and damask rosewater until the mixture turned into a soft paste. This could then be rolled out, shaped and baked.

In his Paste of Genua of Quinces, Plat required the cook to bake the fruit and then dry the mixture in the oven:

> Take Quinces, and peel them, and cut them in slices, and bake them in an Oven dry in an earthen pot, without any other juice than their own: then take one pound thereof, strain it, and put it into a stone mortar with half a pound of sugar and when you have beaten it up to a paste, print it in your moulds, and dry three or four times in an Oven after you have drawn bread, and when it is thoroughly dry and hardened, you may box it, and it will keep all the year dry.

Dried wardens

Henry Butts, ever at odds with everyone else, suggested cutting pears in half, removing the core and then peeling them, before salting and putting them outdoors, presumably to drive out the water to render them better for the constitution. He failed to mention how much salt should be used or how long they should be left outside. Mr Butts advocated preparing the [dehydrated] fruits by sprinkling them liberally with sugar, and either pouring good wine over them, or by cooking them in wine, although this combination of salt and sugar probably did little for the flavour.

Hugh Plat's instructions on 'How to keep Apples, Peares, Quinces, Wardens, etc all the yeare dry' sound as if they would achieve more palatable results. The fruits were to be peeled, cored and cut into thin slices, before being laid out to dry in the sun on either an earthenware or metal dish, or on a high frame covered with coarse canvas. The fruit slices were to be turned occasionally and would keep all year long.

Herring pie

Wardens might occasionally appear in a savoury dish, such as Markham's recipe for a herring pie, when they were added to filleted, white, pickled fish along with raisins, currants, sugar, cinnamon and dates, to give a sweet and sour taste.

Red wardens with a white crust

In 1653, Elizabeth Grey, Countess of Kent recommended how quinces or wardens should be baked so as to present red fruit with a white crust. This was achieved by stewing the wardens in a pipkin (a small earthenware pot or pan) with claret, sugar, cinnamon and cloves, before covering the pipkin with a sheet of pastry and leaving it in the oven for five or six hours. The cook should then make a 'coffin' of pastry and fill it with the cooked wardens and some sugar. This was to be baked for an hour, when it was to be removed from the oven, topped with rosewater and butter, and sprinkled with sugar before returning to bake for a further fifteen minutes. The cooked fruit was to be sprinkled with yet more sugar before serving. Initially this appears to be a sort of 'tart cum pie', but it may be, that she did not intend the pastry 'coffin' to be put on the table.

Street food in Bedford

Although not unique to the county, wardens were popular in Bedfordshire, and Warden Pie is said to have been a delicate dish served at Bedford Borough's municipal banquets. Even as late as the middle of the nineteenth century, the fruit was enjoyed by the general population at the town's Michaelmas fairs where piles of saucers and spoons were provided for the customers, and the pears served from large earthenware pans covered with brown paper. The fruit was also hawked about the streets on autumn evenings, and the local crops must have been enormous if the marketing was anything to go by. Local reports testified to twelve, fourteen or even more boys incessantly shouting for two to three hours every night of the week (except Sundays), 'Hot baked wardens, all hot, in a pot, who knows what I have got, in my pot?'

A lively exchange of opinions took place in the *Correspondence* section of the *Bedford Mercury* starting with a letter dated 29 September 1840 from 'A looker on' who maintained that 'The policemen should be invested with sufficient power, if not wholly, to put a period to this loud jargon - at least, in some manner to regulate the tone, and confine the number of bawlers, to say the most, to three or four'. Some two or three weeks later 'An Independent Man' added 'I am not solicitous to prohibit the sale of wardens, neither do we aim at the extermination of so delicious a dessert as wardens' while going on to complain that the fruit sellers encouraged 'a number of idle boys to follow their train, and add their unmusical notes to the dolerous [*sic*] sound - and thus, by every now and then strengthening their force of bawlers...' The writer sincerely hoped that the mayor would empower the police to stop this 'vexatious nuisance'.

5 Sources

A Book of Cookrye Very Necessary for all such as delight therin. Gathered by A. W. And now newlye enlarged with the serving in of the Table. With the proper Sauces to each of them convenient (printed in London, 1584; repr. 1591)

A proper newe booke of cokerye, ed. C.F. Frere (London, 1545; repr. 1913), pp. 55-56

Amherst, *A History of Gardening in England*, p. 51

Astry, D., 'Diana Astry's Recipe Book c1700', in *Bedfordshire Historical Record Society Vol.37* (Streatley, 1957), p. 153

Austin, T., (ed.), *Two Fifteenth-Century Cookery-Books. Harleian MS. 279 (ab. 1430), & Harl. MS 4016 (ab. 1450) with Extracts from Ashmole MS. 1429, Laud MS. 553, & Douce MS. 55* (London, 1888), pp. 7 and 12-13. The three-part medieval manuscript known as '*Harleian Manuscript number 279*' was written around 1430 A.D. and comprises 153 recipes including 'Wardonys in Siryppe' (also spelled syryp), 'Charde wardoun' (chardewardon) and 'Perys in composte'.

Butts, *Dyets dry dinner*, 'Peares'

Cogan, *The Haven of Health*, p. 125

Culpeper, *The Complete Herbal*, pp. 257-58

Dawson, T., *The Good Huswifes Jewell* (Printed 1587), 'tart of wardens' p. 17 and 'moyse' pp. 33-34 and 38-39

Frazer, Mrs, Confectioner, *The Practice of Cookery, Pastry and Confectionery – in three parts* (Edinburgh, 1820) pp. 238-9

Glasse, H. and M. Wilson, *The Complete Confectioner, Or, Housekeeper's Guide* (London, 1800), p. 71

Goodman, *How to be a Tudor*, pp. 31-32

Greco, G.L., and C.M. Rose (ed. and trans.), *The Good Wife's Guide (Le Ménagier de Paris): A Medieval Household Book* (c.1393) (Cornell University Press, 2009), p. 337 (No. 356)

Grey, Elizabeth, Countess of Kent, *A true gentlewomans delight Wherein is contained all manner of cookery: together with preserving, conserving, drying and candying. Very necessary for all ladies and gentlewomen* (London, 1653), pp. 95-96

Holinshed, R., *Chronicles of England, Scotland and Ireland,* 6 vols., ed. J. Hooker *et al.* (London, 1587; repr. 1807), vol. 1, p. 392

Katharine, A., *Confections and the Banquet* (2007), 'Murrell's Marmelate of Wardens', pp. 4-6, accessed online: www.florilegium.org/files/FOOD-SWEETS/Cft-Banquets-art.rtf

Markham, G., *The English Housewife* (1615), ed. M.R. Best, (MQUP, 1994), 'Herring pie' p. 101, 'Warden pie' p.104, 'paste of Genoa' p.116 and 'Order for serving a banquet' p. 121

Master–Cooks of King Richard II, *Forme of Curye* (*c.* 1390), pp. 64v & 65r. [Digitized by the John Rylands University Library and S. Pegge (printed edition, 1780) accessed online:
http://www.gutenberg.org/cache/epub/8102/pg8102-images.html
http://www.medievalcuisine.com/Euriol/recipe-index/peeres-in-confyt]

Matterer, J.L., 'Pears', in *A Boke of Gode Cookery* (2000), [recipe for roasted wardens (1420)], accessed online:
http://www.godecookery.com/goderec/grec54.htm

Morgan, *The Book of Pears*, p. 116

Norri, J., *Dictionary of Medical Vocabulary in English, 1375–1550: Body Parts, Sicknesses, Instruments, and Medicinal Preparations (London, 2016), p. 191*

Parkinson, *Paradisi in sole paradisus terrestris*, pp. 593-94

Partridge, J., *The Treasurie of commodious Conceits, & Hidden Secrets, and may be called, The huswifes closet, of healthfull provision,* trans. J. Holloway (London, 1573; repr. 2010), 'recipe xxix' accessed online:
http://www.medievalcookery.com/notes/treasurie.pdf.

Plat, H., 'To make a paste to keep you moist', in *Delights for Ladies To adorne their Persons, Tables, Closets and Distillatories: with Beauties, Banquets, Perfumes and Waters* (London, 1609), a.17. See also 'Paste of Genua of Quinces' a.30, 'Marmelade of Quinces or Damsons' a.31 and 'How to keep Apples, Peares, Quinces, Wardens, etc all the yeare dry' a.47

Russell, J., *The Boke of Nurture* (1460/70), ed. F.J. Furnivall (1867), p. 6

Scully, D.E. and T. Scully, *Early French Cookery: Sources, History, Original Recipes and Modern Adaptations* (University of Michigan Press, 2002), p. 14. See also *Du fait de cuisine de Maître Chiquart* accessed online:
http://www.oldcook.com/medieval-maitre_chiquart and
http://doc.rero.ch/record/21865/files/I-N-268_1985_06_00.pdf

The Anglo-Norman Dictionary Online Edition accessed online: http://www.anglo-norman.net/

Woolley, H., *The gentlewomans companion; or, A guide to the female sex containing directions of behaviour, in all places, companies, relations, and conditions, from their childhood down to old age: viz. As, children to parents. Scholars to governours. Single to servants. Virgins to suitors. Married to husbands. Huswifes to the house Mistresses to servants. Mothers to children. Widows to the world Prudent to all. Whereunto is added, a guide for cook-maids, dairy-maids, chamber-maids, and all others that go to service. The whole being an exact rule for the female sex in general* (London, printed 1673), p.155

Woolley, H., 'The Compleat Cook's Guide', in *The Accomplish'd lady's delight in preserving, physick, beautifying, and cookery containing I. the art of preserving and candying fruits & flowers ..., II. the physical cabinet, or, excellent receipts in physick and chirurgery: together with some rare beautifying waters, to adorn and add loveliness to the face and body: and also some new and excellent secrets and experiments in the art of angling, 3. the compleat cooks guide, or, directions for dressing all sorts of flesh, fowl, and fish, both in the English and French mode ...* (London, 1675), 'A Bill of Fare for Autumn, or Harvest', pp. 376-77, and 'Recipe 121. To make a Warden, or Pear-Pye', p. 306

Worde, Wynkyn de, *The Boke of Keruynge* (1508; repr. 1513), in *Early English Meals and Manners,* ed. F.J. Furnivall (London, 1868), pp. 149-74 (pp. 164-166 and 168). This was a textbook on the comportment of polite society and was used by young noblemen who frequently spent time in service in court to learn about such matters.

Recipes

- Baked wardens
- Pear confit
- Wardens in syrup
- Pear compote
- Warden pies

6 Recipes

A taste of the past

Where the recipe recommends a warden, you should use Catillac, Black Worcester or Uvedale's St Germain pears for the most authentic experience. Otherwise, buy the hardest pears you can find for the best results and cook them as soon as possible. Historically, wine was used in most of the recipes, but for non-alcoholic versions, you can use red grape juice instead of red wine, and substitute apple juice for white wine.

As for spicing, cinnamon was popular in the Middle Ages, but you can use ground ginger if you prefer. Where cloves are called for, use them sparingly as they can be overpowering. Better still, experiment with your own flavourings – these medieval recipes were designed with flexibility in mind. Most of all have fun; pears are very forgiving.

Baked wardens

Photos: © M. Roberts

Fruit

1 or 2 pears per person (If baking more than one, select fruits of a similar size.)

Method

1. Pre-heat the oven to 200°C (180°C fan) mark 6.

2. Gently wash the pears in cold water and dry them on kitchen paper. Cut away any damaged flesh and place whole into a large ovenproof dish, or a roasting tin lined with foil. (Ideally the container should be deeper than the pear is tall, to avoid spattering the oven.) Do not cover.

3. Cooking times:

   Wardens: bake for an hour, and then reduce the temperature to 160°C (140°C fan) mark 3 for up to a further 45-60 minutes.

   Other pears: bake for 20-25 minutes, and then reduce the temperature to 160°C (140°C fan) mark 3 for up to a further 20-25 minutes.

To find out whether the fruit is cooked through, push a cocktail stick or thin skewer into the thickest part. If it is done, it will no longer be hard and gritty. The skin will be dark brown and slightly wrinkled.

To serve

The baked warden isn't very appealing, but don't be disheartened, as it has an amazing depth of flavour. Cut in half lengthways, remove the pips and sprinkle with cinnamon and sugar before serving hot or cold; the flesh can easily be scooped out of the skin using a teaspoon. From January onwards, the fruit will be sweeter and you may not need any sugar; simply dust with a little cinnamon.

For other baked pears, it's simpler to peel the fruit and cut it into pieces before sprinkling with cinnamon and serving hot or cold.

Delicious served with some natural yoghurt or crème fraîche.

Pear confit (serves 2-3 as a dessert)

Photo: © M. Roberts

Fruit
2 or 3 pears (about 400-500g (14-18oz))
300ml (½ pint) red wine

Powder blanch
4 teaspoons caster sugar
¼ teaspoon ground ginger
⅛ teaspoon ground cinnamon

Syrup
150ml (¼ pint) dessert wine such as muscat or Vin Santo

Method
1. Remove the eyes from the pears. Peel the fruit, cut away any damaged flesh and place whole into a saucepan. Pour in the red wine.

2. Cover, bring to the boil, then reduce the heat and cook gently until the pears are tender, turning frequently (45–60 minutes for wardens **or** 25 minutes for other pears). Push a cocktail stick or thin skewer into the thickest part of the fruit to check that it is still firm, but no longer hard and gritty. When cooked, leave in the pan to cool slightly with the lid on.

3. In a small bowl, make a 'powder blanch' or spiced sugar by combining the sugar, ginger and cinnamon.

4. Pour the dessert wine into a separate pan and sprinkle in the 'powder blanch' or other preferred combination of spices. Mix well and bring to the boil stirring continuously, then lower the heat and simmer uncovered for 10-12 minutes stirring occasionally. When the mixture has thickened and reduced by about half, transfer the whole, cooked fruits into the pan. Warm them gently for about 5 minutes, spooning over the syrup from time to time.

To serve
Drizzle with syrup and serve warm. Crème fraîche or vanilla ice-cream make a nice accompaniment.

Top Tips

- Reserve the red wine to make pear compote or wardens in syrup. If it's runny, you can add it to Glühwein, but if the liquor has reduced, wait until it is cold and pour it over ice-cream, or add to a crumble or pie filling.

- The cooked pears can be left in the syrup for several hours or overnight to absorb and enhance the flavours. Reheat before serving.

Roasted wardens

Why not experiment with cooking pears over the hottest part of a barbecue, or in the embers of a fire? You might need to protect the bottom of the fruit with a little foil to stop them scorching.

Wardens in syrup (serves 4-6 as accompaniment)

Photo: © M. Roberts

Fruit
2 or 3 pears (about 400-500g (14-18oz))

Syrup
150ml (¼ pint) red wine
1½ tablespoons granulated sugar
½ teaspoon ground ginger
¼ teaspoon ground cinnamon
1 teaspoon malt vinegar
A few threads of saffron

Method
1. Peel and core the pears. Cut away any damaged flesh and place whole into a large saucepan. Cover with plenty of cold water and bring to the boil.

2. Simmer uncovered until tender, topping up with hot water from the kettle as necessary. (The cooking liquor will turn pink and the skin will become slightly wrinkled.) After 30-45 minutes for wardens **or** 10 minutes for other pears, push a cocktail stick or thin skewer into the thickest part of the fruit to check that it is still firm, but no longer hard and gritty.

3. Drain, peel and cut into pieces (about 1cm (½ inch) cubes).

4. Pour the wine into a separate pan and add the granulated sugar, ginger, cinnamon, vinegar and saffron. Bring to the boil stirring continuously, then lower the heat and simmer uncovered for 10-12 minutes, stirring occasionally.

5. When the mixture has thickened and reduced by about half, add the cooked fruit pieces and warm gently until they have slightly softened and changed colour. Check the flavour to ensure that the balance of sweet and sour is to your taste.

To serve
My own experiments have proved that although this dish makes an ideal accompaniment for poultry and fish dishes, it holds no appeal as a dessert to the modern palate. Serve warm or cold with venison, game or poultry.

Top Tips

- The cooked fruit can be left in the syrup for several hours or overnight to absorb and enhance the flavours. Can be reheated.

- If kept in the fridge, return to room temperature before serving.

- The syrup can be prepared ahead and kept at room temperature to allow the spices to infuse before adding the fruit.

Pear compote (serves 2-3 as a dessert)

Photo: © M. Roberts

Fruit
2 or 3 pears (about 400-500g (14-18oz))

Syrup
200ml (⅓ pint) red wine
¼ teaspoon ground cinnamon
½ tablespoon granulated sugar
40g (1½oz) stoned chopped dates
Pinch of salt
1 or 2 teaspoons quince paste, jelly **or** jam (optional)

Method
1. Remove the stalks and eyes from the pears. Peel and cut away any damaged flesh. Place whole into a large saucepan. Cover with plenty of cold water and bring to the boil.

2. Cook uncovered until tender, topping up with boiling water from the kettle as necessary. (The cooking liquor will turn pink.) After 45–60 minutes for wardens **or** 10-12 minutes for other pears, push

a cocktail stick or thin skewer into the thickest part of the fruit to check that it is still firm, but no longer hard and gritty.

3. Drain and allow the fruit to cool slightly, before quartering lengthways, removing the cores and cutting into short, fairly thin slices.

4. In a separate pan, heat together the wine, cinnamon and sugar, stirring until the sugar has dissolved. Do not allow to boil.

5. Remove from the hob and add the dates, cooked pear slices, quince preserve and salt to the wine. Bring to the boil, then reduce the heat and simmer uncovered for about 5 minutes stirring occasionally to ensure that the paste dissolves. Remove from the heat and allow to cool slightly.

To serve
Sprinkle with cinnamon and serve warm or cold with crème fraîche or natural yoghurt. Also great with custard or ice-cream.

Top Tip

- The cooked pears can be left in the syrup for several hours or overnight to absorb and enhance the flavours.

Hannah Woolley's 17th-century Warden Pie (serves 3-4 as a dessert)

Photo: © M. Roberts

Fruit
3 or 4 large pears (about 600-750g (21-26oz))
300ml (½ pint) cold water

Pie
450g (16oz) SR flour
1 level teaspoon salt
140ml (¼ pint) water
150g (5oz) lard

1 tablespoon granulated sugar
Pinch of ground cloves
¼ teaspoon ground cinnamon (more if liked)
1 medium egg, beaten

Method
1. Pre-heat the oven to 160°C (140°C fan) mark 3.

2. Remove the stalks and eyes from the wardens. Peel, core and cut away any damaged flesh. Place whole into an ovenproof dish with the water. Cover and bake for about 4 hours until no longer gritty and hard; the fruit will turn pink or red. Leave to cool.

- For other pears, don't bother pre-cooking; just remove the stalks and eyes, peel and core them.

3. Increase the oven temperature to 200°C (180°C fan) mark 6.

4. Make a rectangular hot water crust pastry case (*a high coffin*) either freehand or in a 1kg (2lb) loaf tin. Make a pastry lid.

5. Put the whole, cooked pears into the pastry case, sprinkle with the sugar, cloves and cinnamon. **For wardens only**, add a little of the cooking liquor. (Other pears don't need the extra liquid.)

6. Brush beaten egg around the top of the pie case and lay the pastry lid on top, sealing firmly using your fingers. Brush the top liberally with beaten egg and make a couple of vents to let the steam out. If baking without a tin, place the pie onto a lined baking sheet. If using a tin, you can put it directly onto your oven shelf. Bake in the centre of the oven for 30 minutes at 200°C (180°C fan) mark 6, reducing to 180°C (160°C fan) mark 4 for 40-45 minutes until the pastry is golden brown.

To serve
Serve warm or cold.

Angela's Warden Pie (serves 4 as a dessert)

Photo: © M. Roberts

If you think life's too short to be making 'high coffins' of pastry, here's an easy alternative for a genuine Warden Pie. You'll need a **20cm (8in) pie dish**.

Fruit

3 large wardens (about 600g (21oz))
1 tablespoon granulated sugar
Pinch of ground cloves, cinnamon, ginger or other spice(s) to taste
Caster sugar for dusting

Method

1. Pre-heat the oven to 160°C (140°C fan) mark 3.

2. Peel, core and slice the fruit and place in an ovenproof dish with just enough water to cover. Sprinkle with sugar and spices.

3. Cover and bake for about 4 hours until no longer gritty and hard. Drain off the excess liquid and reserve to make a jelly or other treat.

4. Increase the temperature of the oven to 220°C (200°C fan) mark 7.

5. Make the pie with your preferred type of pastry (use ready-made if you like). Remember to punch a hole in the top as a vent. Bake for 30-40 minutes until the pastry is cooked through – you don't want a soggy bottom.

To serve
Sprinkle with caster sugar and serve warm or cold, on its own, or with whatever you prefer: ice-cream, cream or custard.

Author's Top Tip

- For even quicker results, instead of baking the wardens for 4 hours, put the sliced fruit into a non-metallic container with a little water and microwave on a medium setting. 10 minutes is enough for one medium-sized fruit, although you won't achieve the same rich colour.

Acknowledgements

I must start by acknowledging the dedication of Jane Markham, manager of Warden Abbey Vineyard and the most patient person I've ever met. Secondly, I'd like to thank Diana Jackson for welcoming me to Eventispress, a not-for-profit, community enterprise supporting local authors; it's a fantastic opportunity for us all. Dr Fiona Steele has done a wonderful job of editing the manuscript and trialling the recipes. Paul Labous of Shuttleworth College has kindly shared the outputs from his research into pear genetics, and I could not have completed the book without help from Old Warden History and Heritage Society members, Angela Little, Richard Batty and Christine Hill. I would also like to recognise the professional advice generously given by food historian, Monica Askay. I am grateful to Fr Erik Varden OSCO and Fr Hilary Costelloe OSCO from Mount Saint Bernard Abbey, Leicestershire for their support and Teresa McKay for her guidance on the Catholic faith. I would finally like to thank Carol Spargo for testing the recipes, and my friends, Dawn and Dave Hill, who have been my colleagues and friends for longer than I can remember.

This work would not have been possible without the materials made available through the following digitisation projects:

- *Internet Archive* https://archive.org/ is a San Francisco based, non-profit digital library, offering free universal access to books, films and music.

- *Google books* https://www.google.com/googlebooks/library/ allows the reader to view and download entire books, which are out of copyright.

- The *Early English Books Online Text Creation Partnership* creates electronic text editions of early printed books. The project is jointly funded and owned by more than 150 libraries worldwide, and the work is released into the public domain for anyone to use. See the University of Michigan interface at http://quod.lib.umich.edu/e/eebogroup/.

- *British History Online* http://www.british-history.ac.uk/ is a not-for-profit, digital library based at the Institute of Historical Research in London. It brings together material for British history from the collections of libraries, archives, museums and academics. The sources, which range from medieval to twentieth century, are easily searchable and browsable online.

Photographic credits

Counterseal attached to Warden Abbey's Deed of Surrender (1537): © M. Roberts, reproduced under licence from The National Archives

Morse depicting the Virgin and child with the abbatial arms (1426/75): By kind permission of The Trustees of the British Museum ©

Uvedale's St Germain pear: © Anne Gilbert / Alamy Stock Photo

Pear trees in Turvey Community Orchard: Reproduced by kind permission of John Warwick